Fantastic Football

OXFORD

UNIVERSITY PRESS

CONTENTS

OXFORD
UNIVERSITY PRESS

Great Clarendon Street, Oxford OX2 6DP

Oxford University Press is a department of the University of Oxford.
It furthers the University's objective of excellence in research,
scholarship, and education by publishing worldwide in

Oxford   New York

Auckland   Cape Town   Dar es Salaam   Hong Kong   Karachi
Kuala Lumpur   Madrid   Melbourne   Mexico City   Nairobi
New Delhi   Shanghai   Taipei   Toronto

With offices in

Argentina   Austria   Brazil   Chile   Czech Republic   France   Greece
Guatemala   Hungary   Italy   Japan   Poland   Portugal   Singapore
South Korea   Switzerland   Thailand   Turkey   Ukraine   Vietnam

Oxford is a registered trade mark of Oxford University Press

Database right Oxford University Press (maker)

First published 2006

British Library Cataloguing in Publication Data

Data available

ISBN-13: 978-0-19-911368-2
ISBN-10: 0-19-911368-8

10 9 8 7 6 5 4 3

Originated by Oxford University Press
Created by BOOKWORK Ltd
All facts are correct at the time of going to press.

Printed in Italy

Diego Forlan,
Uruguay

Kick off

World Cup

Superstars

Club corner

Global game

Oi ref!

Gianluigi Buffon,
Italy

KICK OFF!

Take a patch of grass, 22 players and a leather bag pumped full of air and, hey presto, you have the most exciting and popular team sport on the planet. Football, soccer, *calcio*, *fussball* – whatever you call the game, it is one that is followed by millions upon millions of people.

Nigerian player Rashidi Yekini celebrating a goal in the 1994 World Cup

On 9 April, 1938, the BBC screened the **world's first live television pictures** of a football match – an international between England and Scotland. There were fewer than 20,000 TV sets in the country.

The final of the 2002 World Cup was watched on TV by an estimated **1,100,000,000 people** – almost a sixth of the world's population.

Interest in the game is huge all over the world. In one of Brazil's early 2002 World Cup matches against Belgium, prison warders on the Indonesian island of Sumatra were so busy watching the game that **48 prisoners managed to escape**! Not all of them were recaptured either.

In 1967, both sides in the civil war in Nigeria called a **48-hour ceasefire**. This was so that the great Brazilian striker Pelé could play in an exhibition match in Nigeria's capital city, Lagos.

It doesn't matter how old or young you are, you can still enjoy watching and playing the game. Mexico's Enrique Alcocer joined the Reforma Athletic Club in 1952. He was **still playing** for the club in 2003 **at the age of 79**!

In 2003, Gabriela Ferreira became a football commentator on Brazilian radio – **she was ten years old!**

Way back when

There is no one starting point for football. The game we know today developed from several different pastimes involving some sort of ball and some sort of goal.
In Ancient China, for instance, people played a game called *tsu chu*. They had to **kick and push a stuffed animal skin ball** through 10m-tall bamboo goal posts.

Native Americans played a game called *pasuckuakohowog*, which means '**they gather to play ball with the foot**'. It was reported that the game was played on a 1.6km-long pitch with goals up to 800m wide!

Calcio was played in the 16th century in Italy, but only by **posh aristocrats and popes**. It involved teams of 27 men. Goals were scored by throwing the ball over a certain spot on the edge of the pitch.

In 17th-century Britain, football was played by big mobs and **was often violent**. Many towns banned it and, in 1660, a footballer in Scarborough was put in the stocks.

Charles Wreford-Brown

A game called *aqsaqtuk* was **played on ice** by the Inuit using a ball stuffed with grass, moss and animal hair.

◀ Charles Wreford-Brown is believed to be the first person to use the word soccer as an **abbreviation for association football**, in the 1880s. He later played for England and became vice-president of the English Football Association.

Fame game

Sir Arthur Conan Doyle is famous as the author of **the Sherlock Holmes stories**. It is less known that he played football under the name AC Smith in the 1880s. He was goalkeeper for the English club Portsmouth FC.

The garage band **So Solid Crew**'s Harvey was a youth team player for Chelsea and, in 2003, joined the non-league side AFC Wimbledon.

Spanish singer **Julio Iglesias** was a goalkeeper for Real Madrid, but his career was cut short by a car accident in 1963. While in hospital, he was given a guitar by a nurse, and the rest is musical history.

Record breakers

In 1995, Brazilian striker Ronaldo's ex-wife Milene Domingues smashed the **world record for 'keepy-uppy'**. She kept a football off the ground continuously using her legs, head and body for an amazing nine hours and six minutes.

The world-record for the **longest throw-in** is held, not by a World Cup star, but by English defender Dave Challinor. While playing for Tranmere in 2000, he threw the ball 46.34m – almost half the length of a pitch!

Ghanaian-born football star Ferdie Adoboe is the holder of the world record for the **most touches of a football in 30 seconds** whilst keeping it in the air. He managed 141 touches on the US TV show *Today* in August 2003.

Dave Challinor takes a throw-in

Philosopher and author **Albert Camus** played in goal for Algeria in the 1920s. He once wrote, 'All I know most surely about morality and obligations, I owe to football.'

Singer Rod Stewart signed as an apprentice at English club Brentford in 1960, but **never quite made the grade**.

West Indies cricketer **Sir Vivian Richards** played football as a young man – he even played for Antigua and Barbuda in a qualifying match for the 1974 World Cup.

As a schoolboy, the late pope, **John Paul II**, played in goal for a team in his home town of Wadowice in Poland.

Without fans, football would lack passion and noise. Fans give a game its colour and excitement. Many fans help the club or team they love, not just by paying to watch and cheering them on, but also by volunteering to help out.

English club Shrewsbury Town's ground is next to the River Severn. Before retiring in 1986, Fred Davies used to **fish out all the balls** that were kicked out of the ground into the river. In one season he fished out 130!

Boca Junior supporters at La Bombonera stadium, Buenos Aires, Argentina

Fanatical fans

Jan van Kook was a fan of Dutch side Feyenoord. For the 1998/99 season he bought two season tickets. One was for him and **the other was for his dog** Bo!

During the 2000 European Championships, Dutch police arrested a fan who had **painted his entire rented house orange**, the colours of the Dutch team.

In 2000, Bulgarian Martin Zdravkov had his court application to **change his name to Manchester United** turned down.

Ebby Kleinrensing, a German fan of English side Nottingham Forest, flies from Dusseldorf in Germany to attend every Nottingham Forest game. **It costs him £15,000 a season**. In 2000, he got engaged to Heike Atkinson on the Forest pitch in front of 20,000 fans.

Pedro Gatica cycled all the way from his home in Buenos Aires, Argentina, to Mexico to see Argentina play in the 1986 World Cup. That's **a straight line journey of more than 7,300km**. Unfortunately, he couldn't get a ticket to the game and, while trying to get in, had his bike stolen.

Madcap merchandise

In 1999, Italian club Fiorentina **sold cans of air** taken from its stadium. There were three 'flavours': Air of the Terraces, Essence of Victory and Dressing-room Atmosphere.

In the 2002 World Cup, Japanese player Tsuneyasu Miyamoto wore a black mask to protect his broken nose. Fans copied their hero by **wearing identical masks** to watch Japan's matches. ▶

When Italian club Inter Milan signed Ronaldo in 1997, fake replica shirts bearing his name and his **favourite number 9** went on sale. But the club gave Ronaldo number 10, and then cashed in on sales of the official replica shirts.

Tsuneyasu Miyamoto, Japan

Celebrity selection

Italian side Juventus can count on the actor Omar Sharif, the opera singer Luciano Pavarotti and the American NBA basketball star Kobe Bryant among its celebrity fans. Manchester City has the Gallagher brothers from the band Oasis, while Chelsea has the film maker Lord Attenborough, the actor Sir Michael Caine and the Canadian singer Bryan Adams. Here are a few more celebrity fans:

Celebrity	Team
Arnold Schwarzeneggar	AK Graz (Austria)
Elton John	Watford (England)
Plácido Domingo	Real Madrid (Spain)
Michael Schumacher	Cologne (Germany)
Amir Khan	Bolton Wanderers (England)
Gordon Brown MP	Raith Rovers (Scotland)
Bjorn Borg	Hammarby (Sweden)

Nelson Mandela, South Africa

Make some noise

The Mexican wave, where people cheer and stand up and down one after another around the stadium, is so-called because it became popular at the 1986 World Cup, held in Mexico. Hungarian scientist Dr Tamas Vicsek has measured the average speed of a Mexican wave at 20 seats or 12m per second.

Brazil fans planned a **noisy 'welcome'** for their team, after it crashed out of the 1966 World Cup. The side's manager, Vicente Feola, was **so nervous** that he stayed in Europe for a month before returning home!

The Rapid Quarter Hour is a routine performed by fans of Austrian club Rapid Vienna. For the last 15 minutes of every game, all the **supporters perform fast hand clapping** for up to 15 minutes. No one is quite sure when or why it started, but it has been going on for decades.

Afghanistan fans wishing to cheer and clap their team on when it re-entered international competition in 1998 were in for a shock. The ruling Taliban government declared that '**onlookers will not be permitted to clap**.' Shhhhhhhh.

The best managers and coaches can be crucial to soccer success. But, with fans and the media complaining when the team loses, it can be a high pressure job. Former Spanish star, José Antonio Camacho was appointed manager of Real Madrid in 1998. He walked out after only 23 days!

In a 1999 Spanish league match, Badajoz's Sabino Santos was about to score when the Leganés manager, Enrique Martin, **tackled him**! Martin was banned for ten matches, but Leganés won the game 1-0!

In Belgium, Co Adriaanse was furious that his team, Willem II, **lost 6-1 to Gent**. He made them drive 13km, then run back to the ground!

World Manager of the Year

Arsène Wenger with Thierry Henry

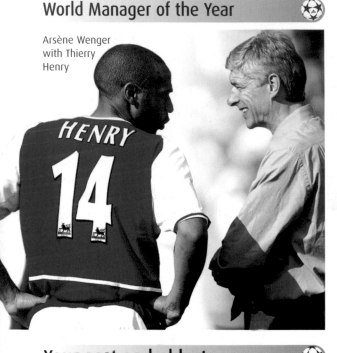

1982	Enzo Bearzot (Italy)
1983	Sepp Piontek (Denmark)
1984	Michel Hidalgo (France)
1985	Terry Venables (Barcelona)
1986	Guy Thys (Belgium)
1987	Johan Cruyff (Ajax)
1988	Rinus Michels (Netherlands & Bayer Leverkusen)
1989	Arrigo Sacchi (Milan)
1990	Franz Beckenbauer (West Germany & Marseille)
1991	Michel Platini (France)
1992	Richard Moller-Nielsen (Denmark)
1993	Alex Ferguson (Manchester United)
1994	Carlos Alberto Parreira (Brazil)
1995	Louis Van Gaal (Ajax)
1996	Berti Vogts (Germany)
1997	Ottmar Hitzfeld (Borussia Dortmund)
1998	Arsène Wenger (Arsenal)
1999	Alex Ferguson (Manchester United)
2000	Dino Zoff (Italy)
2001	Gérard Houllier (Liverpool)
2002	Guus Hiddink (South Korea & PSV)
2003	Carlo Ancelotti (Milan)
2004	José Mourinho (FC Porto & Chelsea)

Youngest and oldest

Bobby Robson (right) and Welshman John Charles, after a match between English and Italian leagues in 1960

Raymond Goethals was **71 years old** when he managed the French club Olympic Marseilles to win the much coveted European Cup in 1993. Unfortunately, the chairman of the club, Bernard Tapie, was **found guilty of corruption** and Marseilles were written out of the record books.

In May 2003, a match between Fulham and Newcastle pitted the **youngest and the oldest managers in the English Premiership** against each other – Chris Coleman (33) and Sir Bobby Robson (70). Sir Bobby began his coaching career with Vancouver Royals in Canada in 1967, three years before Coleman was born!

Juan José Tramutola was **just 27 years old** when he was head coach of Argentina at the 1930 World Cup.

In 2004, **aged 88**, Ivor Verdun Powell helped Team Bath become the first university team to reach the FA Cup first round. He received an award from the English FA for 53 years of coaching.

Record breakers

In Colombia, Gabriel Ochoa Uribe won four league titles as a goalkeeper with the Millonarios club, the first of which was in 1949. He later became a manager and won **another six league championships** with his old side, as well as one with Santa Fe and another seven with América – the last in 1990.

William Struth holds the record for managing one club to the most league championships. He won **18 titles** with Scottish club Rangers between 1920 and 1954.

Carolina Morace was the **first female coach** of a major male team. In 1999, she became coach of Viterbese in Italy's Serie C.

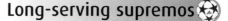
Long-serving supremos

A few managers have been lucky and successful enough to serve for long periods of time without receiving **the dreaded sack.**

◀ Guy Roux became coach of the French club Auxerre in 1961 and, apart from two short breaks, did not leave until his retirement in 2000! His successor Daniel Rolland **lasted only a year** before Roux came back again.

◀ Irishman Martin O'Neill is one of the few managers in major leagues who has **never been sacked**. He started with English club Wycombe Wanderers before moving to Norwich, Leicester City and then Celtic in Scotland, which he left in 2005 to spend time with his family. Experts predict that he will be back in the future.

Sir Alex Ferguson has been sacked only once – from Scottish club St Mirren in 1978, when he **didn't see eye to eye with the chairman**. He has been in charge of Manchester United since 1986, and in 2004 managed the side for the 1,000th game.

Roly Howard should be famous. Why? Because, according to the *Guinness Book of Records*, he is the **longest-serving football manager** at one club. He retired as manager of English Northern Premier League side Marine in 2004/05 after 33 continuous years in charge.

Martin O'Neill celebrating Celtic's Scottish Cup win in 2005

Guy Roux, Auxerre coach

The World Cup is the biggest single-sport event on the planet. Millions upon millions of people follow the highs and lows via television, radio, newspapers and the internet. More than 1.1 billion people – about a sixth of the world's population – tuned in to watch the final of the 2002 competition between Brazil and Germany.

The tournament

The 2002 tournament was filmed by 260 television cameras, which broadcast a **whopping 41,100 hours** of footage. If you had watched it all, it would have taken you more than four and a half years!

Allianz Arena, Munich

The 2006 World Cup Finals will be in Germany. Twelve stadiums will be used, including the **brand new Allianz Arena in Munich**. The see-through walls are fitted with lights to make the stadium glow different colours.

Thirteen teams went to the first World Cup Finals in 1930, but now **more teams want to go** than can be fitted in. They have to qualify from groups around the world.

There are 3.2 million tickets available for the 2006 World Cup, but they are still the **hottest tickets in town**. The official website registered over 9,000 hits every second when one batch of tickets went on sale!

The tickets for the 2006 World Cup Finals come **complete with a computer chip** inside to avoid forgeries. The chips will be read by a special scanner at the stadiums.

Trophy talk

The original **World Cup trophy** was designed by French sculptor Abel Lafleur. It was 35cm high and weighed 3.8kg. The statue was made of sterling silver plated with gold, and the base was made of the semi-precious stone lapis lazuli. In 1950, it was renamed the Jules Rimet Cup.

During the Second World War, an Italian football official, Ottorino Barassi, hid the trophy **under his bed** to stop it from being stolen by soldiers!

In 1970, the Jules Rimet trophy became Brazil's property for ever, because the Brazilians won the tournament for the third time. Unfortunately, **it was stolen** in 1983, and it is rumoured it was melted down. Brazil now has a replica of the trophy.

A staggering 53 designs were considered for the second trophy, the FIFA World Cup. Eventually, a design by Italian artist Silvio Gazzaniga was chosen. The new trophy weighs 4.97kg and has room on its base for 17 winners' names, enough for the trophy to last until 2038.

The new **trophy** is loaned to a winning nation for a short time and remains the property of FIFA. No surprise, because it is made of solid 18-carat gold and is worth about £8 million.

The FIFA World Cup held aloft

Mascot mania

The first World Cup mascot was a lion called **World Cup Willie**, which appeared at the 1966 tournament in England. Since then, there has been a French cockerel (**Footix**), a cheery American dog (**Striker**) and several children.

Other mascots include three robot sculptures from Japan/South Korea (**Kax, Ato and Nik**), a smiling Spanish orange (**Naranjito**) and a Mexican chilli pepper called **Pique**!

The 2006 World Cup mascot ▶ was designed by Jim Henson Workshops, the company behind the TV progammes Sesame Street and the Muppets. Called **Goleo VI**, it is a lion and comes with **Pille**, a talking football that knows lots of facts about the game!

2006 World Cup mascots

WORLD CUP MASCOTS
1966 World Cup Willie
1970 Juanito
1974 Tip & Tap
1978 Gauchito
1982 Naranjito
1986 Pique
1990 Ciao
1994 Striker
1998 Footix
2002 Kax, Ato and Nik
2006 Goleo VI and Pille

Hosts and fans

Japanese fans in 2002

When Brazil was awarded the1950 World Cup, the organisers planned to build the **biggest and best stadium** in the world as the centrepiece. The Maracaná Stadium wasn't ready for the first match, but for the final between Brazil and Uruguay, a staggering 199,950 people crammed into the stadium. It was the biggest attendance at a World Cup match.

Only two other World Cup finals have attracted **an attendance of more than 100,000 people**, and both were held at Mexico's Azteca Stadium, in 1970 and 1986.

Hosts are always granted a place at the **World Cup Finals**. Well, except for Italy in the 1934 tournament. The hosts had to play a qualifying match, which they fortunately won – and went on to win the tournament.

People were worried that the **1994 World Cup** in the USA wouldn't attract enough fans. They need not have done, because 3,587,538 fans watched the matches – more than at any previous World Cup.

The **Fédération** Internationale de Football Association, or FIFA for short, was founded in Paris all the way back in 1904. Serious debate about a world football competition began twenty years later and, mainly due to Frenchman Jules Rimet, the World Cup finally kicked off in 1930. Since that time, it has thrown up lots of great stories.

The Jules Rimet trophy

The 1930s

1930 Only four teams from Europe – France, Yugoslavia, Belgium and Romania – attended **the very first World Cup**. These teams spent two weeks crossing the Atlantic Ocean on the liner *Conte Verde*, picking up the Brazilian team before arriving in Montevideo, the capital of Uruguay.

The 1930 Romanian team wasn't selected by the team manager or coach but by the country's ruler, **King Carol II**.

1934 This World Cup, held in Italy, was the only one at which the **champions didn't defend the trophy**. Uruguay, annoyed by how few European countries had been to its World Cup, refused to send a team to Europe.

At the 1934 World Cup, Swiss striker Poldi Kielholz scored three goals. There was nothing unusual in that, but Kielholz **wore glasses when he played**, which was unusual, and they could have injured him if they had broken.

1938 You have to feel sorry for **Ernst Willimowski of Poland**. He scored four goals in one game against Brazil, but amazingly, he still ended up on the losing side. Brazil won the match 6-5.

When the Italian team, managed by Vittorio Pozzo, won the 1938 World Cup, it became **the first country** to win the World Cup twice in a row, after the country's 1934 triumph on home soil.

The 1950s

1950 The World Cup went on hold in the 1940s because of the Second World War. It started again in 1950, but only 13 teams attended. Uruguay were **the champions**.

1954 Uruguay's Juan Hohberg scored a last-gasp equaliser in the semi-final against Hungary. As his team-mates piled on top of him to celebrate, **Hohberg was knocked unconscious**. He recovered, but Uruguay lost the match 4-2.

West Germany's Fritz and Ottmar Walter are the only brothers to have both scored in the same World Cup Finals match. **The two brothers scored two goals each** in the 1954 semi-final, as West Germany beat Austria 6-1.

1958 This is the only World Cup Finals tournament for which **all four home nations** of the United Kingdom – England, Scotland, Wales and Northern Ireland – qualified.

Ottmar Walter (centre) and Werner Liebrich (right) challenging Ferenc Puskas of Hungary during the 1954 World Cup final

The 1960s

1962 The 1962 World Cup was marred by violence. After only 12 matches, there were four sendings off and 37 injuries including a broken leg and a broken nose. The worst match of all was the '**Battle of Santiago**' between Chile and Italy, in which fighting broke out all over the pitch.

Six players **tied as top scorer** of the 1962 World Cup. Brazilians Garrincha and Vava, the Soviet Union's Valentin Ivanov, Chilean hotshot Leonel Sanchez, Florian Albert of Hungary and Yugoslav striker Drazan Jerkovic all scored four goals.

The England team celebrating in 1966

1966 Disaster loomed just before the first and only World Cup to be held in Britain. The Jules Rimet trophy was stolen whilst on display at a stamp-collecting exhibition at Central Hall in Westminster, London. A week passed before the trophy was found in south London **by a mongrel dog called Pickles**.

England manager Sir Alf Ramsey surprised fans in 1966 by playing a striker, Bobby Charlton, and a defender, Nobby Stiles, in the centre of the England midfield. It did the trick because **England lifted the World Cup**. England won more matches in this World Cup than in all the others it had appeared in previously.

The 1970s

1970 Anatoly Puzach of the Soviet Union became the **first substitute at a World Cup** when he came on for Viktor Serebrjanikov in the first game of the 1970 tournament.

Johan Cruyff in action for the Netherlands

Red and yellow cards made their debut at the 1970 World Cup, but no players were sent off during this tournament. This has not happened since.

A dislocated shoulder did not prevent German legend **Franz Beckenbauer** completing the 1970 World Cup semi-final against Italy. Beckenbauer played the match with his arm strapped to his side.

1974 The final of this World Cup was delayed because, as the teams came on to the field, the referee, England's **Jack Taylor**, spotted that there were no corner flags on the pitch!

The 1974 World Cup was the first tournament in which all the matches were broadcast **on television in colour**.

1978 Robbie Rensenbrink scored the World Cup's **1,000th goal** in 1978. Mind you, his Dutch side ended up losing to Scotland 3-2.

Ernie Brandts, Rensenbrink's Dutch team-mate in 1978, is the only player to have scored a goal and an own goal in the same World Cup match. Fortunately, the Netherlands still beat Italy 2-1.

Ramon Quiroga was Peru's goalkeeper and was nicknamed 'El Loco' for his mad antics. In Peru's match with Poland in 1978, he ran into the opposition's half and got booked for rugby tackling Poland's Gregorz Lato.

The 1980s

1982 Northern Ireland's Norman Whiteside became the **youngest player** to appear in a World Cup Finals. He was 17 years and 42 days old.

Diego Maradona flying through the air after a challenge

When **Alain Giresse** appeared to score a fourth goal for France against Kuwait in 1982, Prince Fahid, the president of the Kuwait FA, **argued with the referee**, who eventually disallowed the goal. France did score a fourth goal and won the game, but the prince was fined £8,000 for his actions.

1986 Diego Maradona of Argentina scored a highly controversial goal against England in the quarter-final. He punched the ball past goalie Peter Shilton into the England net, and the goal stood. While England fans gnashed their teeth, neutrals were thrilled six minutes later when Maradona dribbled the ball more than half the length of the pitch to score one of the finest of all World Cup goals. Maradona later said his first goal was down to '**the hand of god**'.

The 1990s

1990 Cameroon stunned the World Cup holders Argentina in their opening match by beating them 1-0. Cameroon then went on to become the **first African nation to reach the quarter-final stage** of a World Cup.

In the 1990 semi-final between Argentina and Italy, French referee Michel Vautrot forgot all about the time and added on eight minutes during extra-time **by mistake**. Despite playing almost 130 minutes, the two teams drew 1-1. Argentina went through on penalties.

1994 Russia's Oleg Salenko scored five goals in one match against Cameroon – **a World Cup record**. For Cameroon, Roger Milla, at 42 years old, became the oldest player to both appear and score in a World Cup.

The 1994 final was the first to be decided on **penalties.** Brazil beat Italy in the shootout.

1998 This tournament was the largest ever, with 32 teams in the Finals.

Italy's Roberto Baggio after missing the decisive penalty in the 1994 final

The 2000s

2002 This World Cup was **the first to be held in Asia** and the first to be co-hosted by two countries – Japan and South Korea.

The day after the USA were knocked out of the **2002 World Cup**, Landon Donovan was back in the USA, playing for his club, San Jose Earthquakes. The Major League Soccer (MLS) was the only league that did not break its season for the World Cup.

China reached its first ever World Cup in 2002 after many attempts. The team's coach was the Serbian **Bora Milutinovic**, who amazingly had taken four other countries to World Cup Finals before.

Over the years, the World Cup has seen lots of great winners, including Brazilian Mario Zagalo, who won the World Cup as a player in 1958 and then as manager in 1970.

There have also been some **unlucky losers**, such as the German striker Karl-Heinz Rummenigge – the only captain to be on the losing side in the final of two World Cups (1982, 1986).

HIGHEST GOLDEN BOOT WINNERS

The Golden Boot is awarded to each World Cup's highest scorer. Here are the highest scorers of all the Golden Boot winners.

13	Just Fontaine	1958
11	Sandor Kocsis	1954
10	Gerd Müller	1970
9	Ademir	1950
9	Eusebio	1966
8	Ronaldo	2002
8	Leonidas	1938
8	Guillermo Stábile	1930

MOST WORLD CUP FINALS GOALS

14	Gerd Müller 1970, 1974
13	Just Fontaine 1958
12	Pelé, 1958, 1962, 1966, 1970
12	Ronaldo 1998, 2002
11	Sandor Kocsis 1954
11	Jürgen Klinsmann 1990, 1994, 1998
10	Helmut Rahn 1954, 1958
10	Teúfilo Cubillas 1970, 1978
10	Grzegorz Lato 1974 1982
10	Gary Lineker 1986 1990
10	Gabriel Batistuta 1994, 1998, 2002

Gabriel Batistuta, Argentina

World Cup hat tricks

Hat tricks are when a player scores three goals in a single game. Argentina's **Gabriel Batistuta** is the only person so far to score a hat trick at two World Cups, in 1994 and 1998.

The **fastest World Cup hat trick** occurred in just eight minutes in Hungary's 1982 match against El Salvador. The scorer was Laszlo Kiss, who is also the only substitute to score a hat trick.

England's Geoff Hurst remains the only player to have **scored a hat trick in the final** of a World Cup, in 1966.

Just Fontaine wasn't even in France's first team for the 1958 World Cup. An injury to first-choice striker René Bliard gave Fontaine his chance. In his first match **he scored a hat trick** and ended the tournament with 13 goals, the most any player has scored in a single World Cup.

England goalkeeper **Peter Shilton** has had more clean sheets (not let in any goals in a match) at World Cups than any other keeper – ten in three tournaments.

Melanie Hoffmann playing for the German women's team in 1998

Davor Suker, Croatia, (right) won the Golden Boot in 1998, scoring six goals.

Ernst Loertscher of Switzerland will forever be in the record books for scoring the first own goal at a World Cup – during a game against Germany in 1938. Of the **1,803 goals scored in 17 World Cup tournaments**, only 24 have been own goals – just over one per cent.

Only one man has lifted the World Cup as a captain and then won it for a second time as manager. Step forward **Franz Beckenbauer** of Germany. His successes in 1974 and 1990 ensured him a place in the hall of fame.

The World Cup's big winners

WOMEN'S WORLD CUPS			
DATE	HOSTS	WINNERS	RUNNERS-UP
1991	China	USA	Norway
1995	Sweden	Norway	Germany
1999	USA	USA	China
2003	USA	Germany	Sweden
2007	China		

WORLD CUPS			
DATE	HOSTS	WINNERS	RUNNERS-UP
1930	Uruguay	Uruguay	Argentina
1934	Italy	Italy	Czechoslovakia
1938	France	Italy	Hungary
1950	Brazil	Uruguay	Brazil
1954	Switzerland	West Germany	Hungary
1958	Sweden	Brazil	Sweden
1962	Chile	Brazil	Czechoslovakia
1966	England	England	Germany
1970	Mexico	Brazil	Italy
1974	Germany	West Germany	Netherlands
1978	Argentina	Argentina	Netherlands
1982	Spain	Italy	West Germany
1986	Mexico	Argentina	West Germany
1990	Italy	West Germany	Argentina
1994	USA	Brazil	Italy
1998	France	France	Brazil
2002	S. Korea/Japan	Brazil	Germany
2006	Germany		

Yung Hong Duk of Korea holds the unfortunate record for the most goals conceded by a goalkeeper in one World Cup. He let in 16 goals in just two disastrous matches in 1954.

The oldest ever World Cup winner, and the oldest winning captain, was goalkeeper Dino Zoff, who led Italy to World Cup glory in 1982 at the age of 40. The **youngest ever winner** of the World Cup was the fabulous **Pelé**, who was only 17 when Brazil won in 1958.

17

World Cup successes

APPEARANCES IN THE WORLD CUP FINALS

COUNTRY	WINNERS	MADE THE FINAL	MADE THE SEMI-FINALS
Brazil	5	7	10
Germany	3	7	10
Italy	3	5	7
Argentina	2	4	4
Uruguay	2	2	4
France	1	1	4
England	1	1	2
Netherlands	–	2	3
Czechoslovakia	–	2	2
(The Czech Republic and Slovakia)			
Hungary	–	2	2
Sweden	–	1	4
Poland, Yugoslavia, Austria, 2 semi-final appearances each			

WORLD CUP FINALS BIGGEST WINS

1982 – Hungary v El Salvador	10-1
1954 – Hungary v South Korea	9-0
1974 – Yugoslavia v Zaïre	9-0
1938 – Sweden v Cuba	8-0
1950 – Uruguay v Bolivia	8-0
2002 – Germany v Saudi Arabia	8-0

MOST GOALS IN A WORLD CUP FINALS MATCH

12 GOALS

Austria v Switzerland (1954)	7-5

11 GOALS

Brazil v Poland (1938)	6-5
Hungary v West Germany (1954)	8-3
Hungary v El Salvador (1982)	10-1

10 GOALS

France v Paraguay (1958)	7-3

Robert Prosinecki is the only player to have scored goals in the World Cup Finals for **two different teams**. In 1990, he scored for Yugoslavia against the United Arab Emirates. He then scored for Croatia against Jamaica in 1998. (Croatia used to be part of Yugoslavia, but declared its independence in 1991.)

Ronaldo and Kleberson of Brazil

Brazil is the only country to have qualified for or appeared in every single World Cup Finals – that's 18 including the 2006 World Cup, for which the country had to qualify despite being holders.

Chile had a marvellous 1962 World Cup, reaching the semi-finals. The Chileans said **their success was due to food**! They ate Swiss cheese and spaghetti before beating Switzerland and Italy and drank vodka before beating the Soviet Union. Unfortunately, they lost to Brazil in the semi-finals, despite drinking coffee!

In 2002, South Korea became the first Asian side to get to the semi-finals of the World Cup. **The first Asian team** to go to a World Cup Finals was the Dutch East Indies (now part of Indonesia) in 1938.

Including the 2002 World Cup, **Brazil leads the way** with the most goals scored during World Cup Finals. In total, the players have scored a whopping 191 times, more than England, France and Poland combined.

Qualifying for The World Cup

Apart from in 1930, when countries were invited to enter the World Cup, teams have had to qualify for the competition by playing a series of matches against neighbouring countries. So far, 69 different countries have qualified for one or more of the World Cup Finals.

Luis Figo, Portugal

In 2001, Australia posted a World Cup qualifying record score when they beat American Samoa, 31-0 – that's right, thirty-one to nil! Striker Archie Thompson scored only his second goal in international football in the 12th minute. By the time the referee blew his whistle for half-time, he had scored eight. He went on to score 13 goals in the game in just his third ever match for Australia.

Amazingly, given its great football players and clubs of the past and present, **Portugal** has managed to qualify for the World Cup only three times (1966, 1986, 2002). It is one of only three countries (Croatia and El Salvador are the others) that have qualified for two or more World Cup Finals and have not drawn a game at the tournament.

Australia's 31-0 win pleased the Maldives. It meant that the Maldives' 17-0 loss to Iran in 1997 **would no longer be the worst loss** in World Cup qualifying history.

Kharim Bagheri scored **19 goals for Iran** as it qualified for the 1998 World Cup. This is a record for one player in qualifying.

World Cup...whoops!

Colombian goalkeeper René Higuita liked to show off his skills, and in a 1990 match against Cameroon dribbled the ball towards the halfway line. Unfortunately, Higuita stumbled, letting Cameroon striker Roger Milla steal the ball and go on to score the easiest of goals.

Stefan Effenberg

Germany's controversial midfielder **Stefan Effenberg** was substituted early in a game against South Korea in 1994. He made a rude gesture to fans as he left the pitch and was sent home. He didn't play again for the national side for four years.

Mario de Las Casas, once Captain of Peru, is in the record books as **the first player to be sent off at the World Cup**, against Romania in the 1930 tournament.

Poor old Santiago Canizares. He was **Spain's number one choice** going into the 2002 World Cup when he injured himself by dropping a bottle of aftershave on his foot!

19

World Cup shocks are not just in the distant past. In the opening game of the 2002 World Cup, France, the World Cup holders and Euro 2000 champs to boot, were beaten 1-0 by Senegal, a country playing its first ever World Cup Finals game. Papa Bouba Diop's surprise winning goal is just one of many World Cup strikes and shocks.

Hungary were **red-hot favourites** for the 1954 World Cup, especially after they scored a staggering 17 goals in their first two games. In the final, they came up against West Germany, one of the sides they had thrashed. West Germany had the last laugh though. The manager had fielded a weakened side in the early game, and the West Germans **came out surprise winners** of the final.

Hungary's goalkeeper Gyula Grosics in the 1954 World Cup final

The Norway team celebrating victory over Brazil

Norway looked **down and out** in the 1998 World Cup when mighty Brazil went 1-0 up with just 12 minutes to go. But **the Norwegians rallied**, and goals by Tore Andre Flo and Kjetil Rekdal secured an unlikely victory.

Bulgaria had a **lousy record at World Cups**. They had not won a game in five World Cups (1962, 1966, 1970, 1974 and 1986). At the 1994 Finals the team lost its first match, but boy did they improve – beating Greece, Argentina, Mexico and the defending champions, Germany, to reach the semi-finals. Iordan Letchkov remains **a hero in Bulgaria** for his spectacular diving header, which won the game against Germany.

Bulgaria's Iordan Letchkov scoring against Germany

South Korea's captain Myung Bo Hong celebrating the winning penalty against Spain in 2002

Underdogs make good

Group A at the 1958 World Cup contained four teams: Argentina, West Germany, Czechoslovakia and Northern Ireland, but that wasn't the order in which the four sides finished. Argentina and West Germany were knocked out and Northern Ireland, **the smallest nation ever to qualify for the Finals**, topped the group!

The players of **Costa Rica** had a fine time at their first ever World Cup in 1990, beating Scotland 1-0 and Sweden 2-1.

Cuba stunned Romania at the 1938 World Cup by holding them to a 3-3 draw. **Worse was to come for the Romanians** in the replay. This time Cuba beat them 2-1.

England's first World Cup appearance was in 1950. It wasn't a happy one as they were surprisingly beaten 1-0 by the USA. Some **newspapers back in Britain didn't believe the news** and printed that the score was USA 1 England 10!

Larry Gaetjens, **the scorer of the USA's winning goal** against England in 1950, was born in Haiti. He worked in a restaurant at the time, cleaning dishes.

Algeria made its debut at the 1982 World Cup, and the team was not highly rated. But the football experts got it wrong, because **Algeria beat a strong West German team** 2-1 in one of the all-time World Cup surprises. Sadly for the Algerians, West Germany and Austria played out an uncompetitive game in the group to ensure they both qualified for the next round and Algeria did not.

Shocks from Korea

⬤ The South Koreans gave their home fans plenty to cheer about at the 2002 World Cup. The Asian side, which many pundits thought would lose every match, **knocked out three genuine European giants**, Portugal, Italy and Spain, to make the semi-finals – an amazing feat.

North Korea had provided the shock of the 1966 tournament. With a goal from **Pak Doo Ik**, North Korea knocked the Italians out of the World Cup. The Italian players were pelted with rotten fruit and vegetables when they arrived home!

There was very nearly another Korean shock in the next round in 1966. After a stunning 20 minutes, North Korea led one of the tournament favourites, Portugal, 3-0. But they couldn't hold on and Portugal, **inspired by Eusebio**, won 5-3.

21

The great game of football has made superstars out of some of its very best players. Awards, fame and glamour follow football greats like Pelé, Zidane, Raul and Beckham, who draw huge crowds wherever they go.

The 2005 **Football For Hope** match between a World XI and a Europe XI was watched by millions of people on TV. The match was to raise money for the victims of the Asian tsunami. The transfer value of all the players on view was almost £1 billion!

Hidetoshi Nakata is undoubtedly Japan's most famous and well-paid player. In 2003, when playing for **Italian club Parma**, he was paid an estimated ¤9.3 million (£6 million) a year, the same as the top Spanish striker, Raul.

People discuss top players in some high places. In 1998, an argument broke out in the Italian parliament about whether Ronaldo should have won a penalty when Inter Milan played Juventus. It ended in a **fight between two MPs**!

David Beckham, England

Mia Hamm from the USA is the most **famous female footballer** – so famous that sports company Nike named their main office building in Oregon, USA, after her!

Mia Hamm, USA

Beckham bonanza

Although not the world's best player, David Beckham may well be the world's most famous. What other player has a **Buddhist temple in Thailand** dedicated to him, as well as a university course in England about him called David Beckham Studies?

Beckham missed a penalty against Portugal at the **Euro 2004 Championships**. The fan who grabbed the ball auctioned it on a website. The ball sold for £19,000!

In Japan, Beckham is known as Beckham-Sama which means Prince Beckham. On a visit to Japan in 2003, he was greeted by a 3m-high **statue of himself made out of chocolate**!

The Villette family from Northamptonshire were such big Manchester United fans that, in 1999, they **named their third son Beckham**. His brothers are called Ince and Cantona after two other former United players.

Long, hard work

Behind the glamour of being a professional footballer lies a lot of hard work. A **computer video study** of midfielders from Euro 2004 figured out that an attacking midfielder like Zidane of France or Figo of Portugal runs more than 11.2km in one match.

In a long professional career, a top player can easily play more than 700 competitive matches. That means a top midfielder will **run 7,840km** – that's about the same as running from England to China – and that doesn't include any training!

On November 11th 1987, Welsh striker Mark Hughes played for **Wales against Czechoslovakia** during the day, then flew to Munich, Germany, to play for his club, Bayern Munich in the evening.

Dutch star Dennis Bergkamp is really scared of flying. When his club, Arsenal, played the Italian side Fiorentina in the Champions League in 1999, he did the 1,760km journey by car, **taking two days to get to the game**!

Dennis Bergkamp, the Netherlands

FIFA World Player of the Year

The coaches and captains of national teams all around the world vote for the FIFA world player award – **the ultimate accolade for any footballer**. Brazil's Ronaldo and France's Zinedine Zidane are the only players to have won it three times.

1991	Lothar Matthäus (Germany)
1992	Marco van Basten (Netherlands)
1993	Roberto Baggio (Italy)
1994	Romario (Brazil)
1995	George Weah (Liberia)
1996	Ronaldo (Brazil)
1997	Ronaldo (Brazil)
1998	Zinedine Zidane (France)
1999	Rivaldo (Brazil)
2000	Zinedine Zidane (France)
2001	Luis Figo (Portugal)
2002	Ronaldo (Brazil)
2003	Zinedine Zidane (France)
2004	Ronaldinho (Brazil)

Ronaldo, Brazil

Awards

Jürgen Klinsmann, Germany

The first player to win the English **Footballer of the Year award** who was not from England, Ireland, Scotland or Wales was German striker, Jürgen Klinsmann in 1995. He was playing for Tottenham Hotspur.

The first winner of the English Footballer of the Year award was **Sir Stanley Matthews** in 1948. He also became the oldest professional footballer in England when he turned 50 years old and continued to play.

France's brilliant midfielder Michel Platini is the only player ever to win **European Footballer of the Year** three times in a row. He won the award in 1983, 1984 and 1985.

◀ Sometimes football superstars attract unwanted attention. Alfredo di Stefano from Argentina was one of the **best players in the world** in the late 1950s and early 1960s. In 1963, he was kidnapped in Venezuela but was released unharmed after a couple of days.

Alfredo di Stefano, Argentina

Dutch midfield star Edgar Davids is famous for wearing special protective glasses while playing, after he had operations on his eyes for glaucoma. **Jef Jurion**, who played 63 times for Belgium during the 1960s, also wore glasses while playing.

When is a superstar not a superstar? When he's a fake! In 1996, Graeme Souness signed **Ali Dia** on a 30-day contract after the great African striker **George Weah** had recommended him over the phone. The caller wasn't Weah, however, and Dia was no superstar player. This became clear within minutes of him going on the pitch!

Early days

◀ Born in 1940, the great Pelé grew up in the town of Três Corações. **He shined shoes** to help his family make ends meet, until he was spotted as a footballing talent.

Pelé, Brazil

Peter Schmeichel of Denmark was one of the best goalkeepers in the world, but as an amateur he was a striker. He showed off his goal-scoring skills in a UEFA Cup game against Rotor Volgograd, in 1995, when he was Manchester United's goalie. He came up for an attack and scored!

English striker Ian Wright didn't ▶ start playing professional football until he was 22. He had trials with south London schools, and clubs Millwall and Brighton, but he **was rejected each time**. He eventually began his professional career with Crystal Palace in 1985, then moved to Arsenal where he was top scorer for six seasons in a row.

Ian Wright's son also **suffered rejection**. He was released by Nottingham Forest at the age of 16 and was eventually signed by Manchester City. He is now an England star and was sold to Chelsea in July 2005 for £21 million.

A muddy training session for Ian Wright (left) and fellow England star Paul Gascoigne

24

Keeping it in the family

Ian Wright and Shaun Wright-Phillips are not the only father and son footballers. Frank Lampard and Frank Lampard Jr both **started their careers at West Ham**. Frank Jr now plays for Chelsea and is an England star.

In Italy, the most famous father and son have to be **Cesare Maldini and his son, Paolo**. Both played for AC Milan. Paolo Maldini has remained at the club for his entire career and became Italy's most-capped player. Cesare Maldini became manager of the Italian national team – and managed his son at the 1998 World Cup Finals.

Cesare (left) and Paulo Maldini

There have been lots of brothers who have **played together in the national side**. Three of the most famous were the English World Cup winning Charltons, Jackie and Bobby, Denmark's Michael and Brian Laudrup (their father, Finn Laudrup was also a professional footballer) and the Dutch brothers, Frank and Ronald de Boer.

During the 1970s, Klaus Sammer played 17 times for East Germany. His son, Matthias, is **one of the few players** who played for East Germany and the reunited Germany.

Bobby and Jackie Charlton, playing against each other in the English league

Michel Platini, France

French legend Michel Platini was rejected by Metz at 16 after a medical showed he had a weak heart. Platini trained hard and become the captain of France, **inspiring his country** to their first European championship in 1984.

'**Look at that little fat chap. We'll murder this lot**,' said one unnamed England player as the team lined up against Hungary in 1953. The little fat chap was none other than the football legend Ferenc Puskas. He dazzled as Hungary humbled England 6-3 and then thrashed them 7-1 in a return match.

Bouncebackability

After making a blunder in his first league game for Moscow Dynamo, and letting in four goals in his next, Russian Lev Yashin was put in the reserves for two years, **before getting another chance**. He soon became the best keeper in the world and helped the Soviet Union win the 1960 European Championships.

Welsh star Ryan Giggs was rejected by Manchester City at 14, so in 1987 **he went across town** to join United. England's Kevin Keegan was rejected by Coventry City at the same age in the 1960s, but he went on to international fame.

If you are small for your age, don't let people tell you you can't play football! Denmark's Allan Simonsen was so small his nickname was '**the flea**', but he went on to become European Footballer of the Year in 1977.

Goals are what the game is all about. You can't win games without scoring goals, and players who score goals regularly are the most valued and highly paid footballers. Pelé was one of the best scorers of all time. In 1,324 professional games, he scored a staggering 1,282 goals.

Gerd Müller,
West Germany

Goalscoring legends

🔺 Gerd Müller was signed by the German club Bayern Munich in 1964 against the wishes of the coach Tschik Cajkovski, who said, '**I don't want that elephant amongst my thoroughbreds.**' Gerd Müller went on to break club and country goalscoring records, bagging 628 goals in total, and still leads the World Cup goalscorers' table with 14 goals.

Coach Bela Guttman **discovered his greatest signing**, for the Portuguese club Benfica, at the barbers in 1961. He bumped into a fellow manager, who told him about one of his young strikers called Eusebio. Guttman swooped in and signed Eusebio for his club. Eusebio scored an incredible 317 goals in 291 appearances for Benfica.

Gunnar Nordahl scored 44 times in just 30 games for Sweden in the 1940s. In his eight seasons at Italian team AC Milan, he was Serie A's **top scorer five times**. He remains AC Milan's leading scorer, with 210 goals.

Franz Binder is one of the **great goal machines** Between 1930 and 1950, he played for Austria 19 times, scoring 16 goals, and for Germany 9 times, scoring 10 goals. He was the first European to score over 1,000 goals.

Top scorers

Romário de Souza Faria has been **top scorer in three different countries** – his native Brazil, the Netherlands and Spain. He holds the record for the most times he has been the season's leading goalscorer in a major league – a whopping 13! He now plays for Brazilian club Vasco da Gama.

🔻 Alan Shearer holds the record for the **most goals scored** in the English Premier League – 250 by the end of the 2004/05 season.

Alan Shearer,
Newcastle

Highest goalscorers (selected countries)

Country	Scorer	Goals	Country	Scorer	Goals
Argentina	Gabriel Batistuta	56	Mexico	Carlos Hermosillo	35
Brazil	Pelé	77	Netherlands	Patrick Kluivert	40
Czech Republic	Jan Koller	34	Northern Ireland	David Healy	16
Denmark	Poul Nielsen	52	Rep. Ireland	Robbie Keane	24
England	Bobby Charlton	49	Russia	Vladimir Beschastnykh	26
France	Michel Platini	41	Portugal	Eusebio	41
Germany	Gerd Müller	68	Scotland	Denis Law/Kenny Dalglish	30
Greece	Nikolaos Anastopoulos	29	Spain	Raul	41
Hungary	Ferenc Puskas	84	Sweden	Sven Rydell	49
Italy	Luigi Riva	35	Turkey	Hakan Sukur	46
Japan	Kazuyoshi Miura	56	USA	Eric Wynalda	34

Iran's Ali Daei holds the world record for most goals for a country. He has scored a whopping 106!

Brazilian Rivelino scored an extraordinary goal at the 1974 World Cup. He struck the ball straight at his team mate Jairzinho, who was in the East German wall. Jairzinho **ducked with perfect timing** and the ball sailed through the small gap in the wall into the net.

In the 2003/04 season, the **highest goalscorer** in the whole of Europe was Armenia's Ara Hakobian. He scored 45 goals for his club Banants Yerevan.

When it comes to scoring goals, Brazilians seem to be the best. By the end of his career in 1934, Arthur Friedenrich is believed to have scored **1,329 goals**.

Whoops! Own goals

The very last goal at Bayern Munich Olympiastadion ground in 2005 was an own goal. But the home fans were happy – it was **scored by their opponents** and Bayern won 6-3.

Most own goals are deflections or occur close to goal. Not Zoran Mirkovic's during a 1997 Italian league match against Atalanta. He fell as he was about to hit a flying ball and **sent it over his own keeper** from 30m away!

Zoran Mirkovic playing for Juventus in Italy

In 1976, Chris Nichol, playing for Aston Villa in England, **scored all four goals** in a game against Leicester City. The final score was 2-2!

In Brazil, in 1982, Jorge Nino wasn't too popular with his Democrata team-mates. He scored a **hat trick of own goals** for rivals Atletico Mineiro.

The most own goals scored in one match, and the most goals of any sort to have been scored in one match, is 149! In 2002, in Madagascar, AS Adema players watched in astonishment as their opponents, Stade Olympique l'Emryne, **scored own goal after own goal**. It was a protest against refereeing decisions in an earlier game.

When Cambridge United kicked off a match in England in 1977, Ian Seddon **sent a high ball** towards Torquay United's penalty area. Torquay defender Pat Kruse leapt high to head the ball – past his keeper into his own net. This is the fastest recorded own goal – under six seconds!

Celebrations

Goal celebrations used to be a gentlemanly shake of the hand or pat on the back. Now they are more like a scene from a circus or a gymnastics competition. Ecuadorian striker Facundo Sava keeps a **Zorro-style mask** in his sock, which he pulls out and wears after scoring a goal.

In England, Thierry Henry scored against Chelsea in 2000. He ran to the corner to start celebrating and **hit himself in the face with the corner flag**! Italian star Marco Tardelli did a similar thing at the 1982 World Cup.

Argentine striker Martin Palermo scored in extra time for Villareal in the Spanish Cup in 2001. He rushed over to share his excitement with the fans, but **a pitch-side wall collapsed on him**. He broke two bones in his leg and wasn't able to play football again for six months. Ouch!

Before making his Premier League debut for Chelsea in 1997, Celestine Babayaro played in a pre-season match, scored and **attempted a somersault** to celebrate. He broke a bone and didn't play again for Chelsea for months.

Julius Aghahowa of Nigeria celebrating a goal

Hat trick heroes

In 1998, Masashi Nakayama scored a hat trick for his Japanese club Jubilo Iwata – in **four games in a row**! He scored five goals in the first match, four in the second and third matches and three in the fourth match.

The **fastest hat trick** in top-flight football was scored by Argentine Eduardo Maglioni, in 1973. He got three goals in one minute and 50 seconds.

Defenders with most goals

GOALS	NAME	COUNTRY	GAMES	DATES
193	Ronald Koeman	Netherlands	533	(1980-1997)
134	Daniel Passarella	Argentina	451	(1974-1989)
110	Fernando Hierro	Spain	530	(1987-2004)
108	Egardo Bauza	Argentina	499	(1977-1992)
103	Paul Breitner	Germany	369	(1970-1983)

Damien Mori, Australia

Speedy strikes

The fastest goal of all time is believed to have been scored by Australian Damien Mori of Adelaide City, when playing against Sydney United in a 1995 game. According to FIFA, the goal was scored **just 3.67 seconds into play**!

England's Bryan Robson scored against France in the 1982 World Cup after just 27 seconds. This was the record for the **fastest ever World Cup Finals goal**, and Robson held it for 20 years. At the 2002 World Cup third place play-off, Turkey's Hakan Sükür **struck after only 11 seconds** to break the record.

Who is the scorer of the **fastest international goal**? Is it Pelé or Ronaldo of Brazil, Klinsmann or Müller of Germany or Raúl of Spain? No, it's San Marino's Davide Gualtieri, who scored with just 8.3 seconds on the clock in a World Cup qualifying match in 1993. His opponents were England – who failed to qualify.

Tunisia's Zoubeir Beya leading his team-mates in celebration after beating Zambia 4-2 in the semi-final of the African Nations Cup in 1998

Goal feasts ✪

The record for the highest score in senior football was held by Scottish club Arbroath, who thrashed Bon Accord 36-0 in 1885. This record was smashed in 2002 (see p27).

Top women goalscorers ✪

Scorer	Goals	Country
Mia Hamm	158	USA
Elisabetta Vignotto	107	Italy
Carolina Morace	105	Italy
Michelle Akers	105	USA
Kristine Lilly	101	USA
Tiffeny Milbrett	100	USA
Sun Wen	94	China
Birgit Prinz	88	Germany
Heidi Mohr	83	Germany
Julie Fleeting	78	Scotland

The biggest win in a major European cup competition occurred in 1984. Dutch side **Ajax beat the Red Boys Differdange** from Luxembourg 14-0 in the UEFA Cup.

Stephan Stanis of Racing Club Lens scored 16 goals in a single French Cup game in 1942. The victims were Aubry-Asturies. This is **a world record** for a senior professional match.

English club Liverpool came back from 3-0 down to Italian AC Milan to win the 2004/05 Champions League. And there have been other **amazing come-backs**. Imagine you're a Charlton Athletic fan in England in 1957. Your side are 5-1 down to Huddersfield Town and, if that isn't enough, your team is down to ten men. There's only half an hour to go so **you might as well go home**. Wrong! Charlton went on to win 7-6.

29

Goalies are different. They wear different kit to their team-mates and are the only players allowed to handle the ball. Before 1912, keepers were allowed to handle the ball anywhere in their own half. A few keepers even scored goals by throwing the ball into the opponents' net!

Some people think that you **have to be a bit mad** to be a keeper. They point to goalies like Welsh international Leigh Richmond Roose, who played in the early 1900s. He always wore the same unwashed lucky undershirt beneath his goalie's jersey. Pooh!

Gianluigi Buffon,
Italy

Italian keeper Gianluigi Buffon became the world's most expensive goalie in 2001, when he moved to Juventus from Parma for £32.6 million. Gianluigi comes from **a very sporting family**: his father, Adriano, was a junior weightlifting champion; his mother, Stella, represented Italy at discus throwing; his sisters, Guendalina and Veronica, play for Italy's national volleyball team.

Chelsea's first ever captain was a goalkeeper who was also the world's heaviest footballer. **William 'Fatty' Foulke** was signed from Sheffield United for £20 in 1905. He weighed in at over 135kg. Team-mates used to take the mickey out of him for his weight, but he would get his own back by sitting on a player until he apologised!

What do you do if your dad is the world's most famous striker? Well Edinho, the son of Brazilian legend Pelé, decided to be a goalkeeper. And he was a good one too, becoming the first-choice keeper at his father's old club, Santos.

Goalie Jesus Angoy won the 1992 European Cup with Barcelona. But by 1999 he had **switched sports** to play American football with the **Denver Broncos**.

Scottish goalkeeper Andy Goram also played cricket for Scotland three times. His first match was against Australia in 1989. Fast bowler Merv Hughes bowled him a bouncer then told him to **stick to football**!

Moscow Dynamo's **Lev Yashin** is the only goalkeeper to be European Footballer of the Year (1963). The great Russian keeper was called 'the black panther'.

Gordon Banks, England goalkeeper in the 1960s and 70s, didn't use gloves until near the end of his career. He used to **chew gum** and use the sticky saliva on his fingers to give him extra grip.

Walter Scott of the English club Grimsby Town was the first person to **save three penalties** in one match. He performed this amazing and heroic feat in 1909 against Burnley.

Goalscoring goalies

Imagine a goalkeeper being his club's top scorer in a season! Well, it happened in the 1999/2000 season when German goalie Hans-Jorg Butt **scored nine goals** for the famous German side, SV Hamburg.

José Luis Chilavert taking a free kick against Japan, 2001

⬤ The king of goalscoring goalkeepers is Paraguay's José Luis Chilavert. The fiery keeper regularly takes penalties and free kicks for his club and country. He has racked up 62 goals – 45 from penalties, 15 from free kicks, and two in open play when he joined in an attack!

World goalkeepers of the year

1987	Jean-Marie Pfaff	Belgium
1988	Rinat Dasaev	Soviet Union
1989	Walter Zenga	Italy
1990	Walter Zenga	Italy
1991	Walter Zenga	Italy
1992	Peter Schmeichel	Denmark
1993	Peter Schmeichel	Denmark
1994	Michel Preud'homme	Belgium
1995	José Luis Chilavert	Paraguay
1996	Andreas Köpke	Germany
1997	José Luis Chilavert	Paraguay
1998	José Luis Chilavert	Paraguay
1999	Oliver Kahn	Germany
2000	Fabien Barthez	France
2001	Oliver Kahn	Germany
2002	Oliver Kahn	Germany
2003	Gianluigi Buffon	Italy
2004	Gianluigi Buffon	Italy

Ouch!

Perhaps the strangest injury to a goalkeeper came in a 1975 match featuring Manchester United keeper Alex Stepney. He had to leave the field **after dislocating his jaw** while shouting at his defenders! There was no substitute goalie, so midfielder Brian Greenhoff had to go in goal, and he managed to keep a clean sheet.

Clean sheets

Not letting in a goal is known as keeping a clean sheet. Every goalie aims to keep a clean sheet for as long as possible. Italian keeper Walter Zenga holds **the record in the World Cup**, going 517 minutes (almost six games) in the 1990 competition without conceding.

The longest known record for keeping a clean sheet in professional football is held by **Spanish keeper Abel Resino** of Atletico Madrid. He went 1,275 minutes (more than 14 matches) in 1990/91 without letting in a goal.

In international football, Italian Dino Zoff holds the record for the longest-lasting clean sheet, going an astonishing 1,142 minutes (**more than 12 matches**) without a goal being scored against him. Can you guess which nation broke Zoff's record? Was it mighty Brazil, France, Argentina? Nope, it was Haiti with a goal by Sanon in the 1974 World Cup Finals.

Italy's goalkeeper Walter Zenga saving a shot from Argentina's Oscar Ruggeri

Manchester City's German goalkeeper Bert Trautmann was injured during the 1956 FA Cup final. He bravely played on, **helping his side to a 3-1 victory**. It was only afterwards that Trautmann discovered he had broken his neck!

US goalkeeper Kasey Keller needed an unscheduled trip to the dentist in 1998, but it was **nothing to do with playing football**. He knocked out his front teeth while pulling his golf bag from his car!

The very first football club was Sheffield FC, which was formed in the mid-1850s. By the time the first football association was founded in 1863, 12 clubs attended. Today, there are thousands of clubs all over the world.

Manchester United are considered **the most supported club in the world**. The official supporters club has 152,000 members and a further 45,000 season ticket holders. In 2001/02, an opinion poll found that as many as 50 million people around the world followed the team.

Czech Republic side Bohemians is nicknamed the Kangaroos, although it is based about 13,000km from Australia. The club toured Australia in 1927 and was presented with **two live kangaroos**! The kangaroos were taken to Prague Zoo and the club put a kangaroo symbol on its team badge.

Some very famous club colours were once quite different. Juventus now play in black and white stripes, but **first played in pink shirts**. Liverpool spent their first five years not wearing red, but blue and white quarters. Up until the 1960s, Leeds United wore a blue and gold strip before manager Don Revie changed it to an all-white strip **to mimic the great Spanish side** Real Madrid.

Total Network Solutions' Martyn Naylor tackles Liverpool's Xabi Alonso, 2005

Name changes

In 1996, Llansantffraid won the Welsh Cup and **changed its name to that of its sponsor**. The team, now called Total Network Solutions FC, plays in the League of Wales and were knocked out of the 2005/06 Champions League by Liverpool.

Any ideas who **Dial Square**, **Newton Heath** and **Thames Iron Works** are? They were the original names of three famous English teams: Arsenal, Manchester United and West Ham United.

What's in a name?

A number of teams from all over the world have chosen their club name in tribute to an older, European team. Here are eight great examples:

Ajax Cape Town (South Africa)
Arsenal Kyiv (Ukraine)
Benfica (Namibia)
Liverpool (Uruguay)
Chelsea (Namibia)
Barcelona (Ecuador)
Manchester United (Gibraltar)
Club Valencia (Maldives)

In Germany, a number of teams include the date of when their club was founded or merged with other clubs in their name. Examples include:

Schalke 04
Bayer 04 Leverkusen
FSV Mainz 05
Hannover 96

Around the world, there are some great, if strange, names for football clubs. Here are seven unusually named teams who have enjoyed success in their country:

Violent Kickers (Jamaica) – league champions 1994, 1996
FC Dodo (Mauritius) – league champions 1970
Robin Hood FC (Surinam) – league champions 1983-1989
Hallelujah (South Korea) – league champions 1983
Eleven Men In Flight (Swaziland) – cup winners 2001
Inter Bom-Bom (Sao Tome & Principe) – league champions 2000
Flying Camel (Taiwan) – five times league champions

Derby dramas

Barcelona's Luis Enrique (left) scoring against Real Madrid's goalkeeper Dominguez Cesar

Derby matches are passionate games between two rival clubs, often from the same city or area. There are some very big derbies around the world, such as Celtic v Rangers in Scotland, Real Madrid v Barcelona in Spain and Boca Juniors v River Plate in Argentina.

The rivalry between Egypt's two biggest clubs, Zamalek and Al Ahly is so fierce that a foreign referee is often brought in for these derby matches. In 2001, Scotland's Kenny Clark was chosen to referee after six other European countries had **refused to send a ref**.

Some clubs have a **long way to travel** for their nearest match. In Norway, Tromso play their 'local' derby against Bodo Glimt. The two teams are 410km apart.

In Australia's new A-League, the closest thing to a derby match for Perth Glory will be Adelaide United. The two are **separated by more than 2,150km**!

In 1991, during Uruguay's big derby match between Peñarol and Nacional, Nacional's Dely Valdez was **robbed of a gold chain while he was playing**! The player himself and those in the ground didn't spot the thief, but the TV cameras did. During a tussle at a corner, Peñarol defender Goncalves had ripped off the chain and **hidden it in his sock**! He was arrested by police straight after the game, and handed the chain back.

Every **country** that plays football has a league system. The five biggest leagues in the world are all based in Europe. They are Serie A (Italy), English Premier League, Bundesliga (Germany), La Liga (Spain) and Le Championnat (France).

Serie A

From 1929, when Serie A started, to the end of the 2004/05 season, Juventus were the **most successful club**. They won 2,392 out of 3,199 games and 27 league championships. In those games, they **scored 4,114 goals**.

AC Milan and Inter Milan both play at the San Siro stadium. They are the **second and third most successful** Serie A teams, with 17 and 13 Serie A titles, or *scudettos*, respectively.

In the 1993/94 season, Lecce were relegated with **just 11 points**, 39 points behind the winners (Milan).

Andriy Shevchenko, AC Milan

Romanian Florin Raducioiu (left) has played in the top division of all five big European leagues

Le Championnat

On 15 April, 1976, Nantes began an **unbeaten run** in home games that did not end until April 1981 – a total of 92 games.

AS Saint-Etienne have **won more league titles** than any other French club – a grand total of ten. But their **last win** came in 1981.

Lyons was founded in 1950, but didn't do well in the French league until 1995, when they came second. They followed up with **three straight league titles** in 2002, 2003 and 2004.

Bundesliga

There have been six German Bundesliga games in which one side has **scored ten or more goals**. Borussia Mönchengladbach hit ten four times, the last in 1984.

Germany's top division is the best-supported in the world, averaging **37,565 fans per match** in 2004/05.

Tasmania Berlin will be remembered as **the worst performing club**. In August 1965, the team won the first game of the season in front of 81,000 fans. Their next win was in May 1966, in front of just over 2,000 die-hard supporters.

La Liga

Barcelona **resisted having any advertising** on their strip until 2005. They then agreed to use the logo of television company TV3 – but only on one arm of the shirts.

In 1951/52, Atlético Tetuán – **a side from northern Morocco** played in La Liga. This is because part of Morocco was under Spanish control at the time.

MOST LEAGUE CHAMPIONSHIPS WON BY A EUROPEAN CLUB	
51	Rangers FC (Scotland)
44	Linfield FC (N. Ireland)
38	Celtic (Scotland)
34	AC Sparta Prague (Czech Republic)
31	Olympiakos (Greece)
31	Rapid Vienna (Austria/Germany)
30	SL Benfica (Portugal)
28	Ajax (Netherlands)
28	CSKA Sofia (Bulgaria)
28	Real Madrid (Spain)
27	Ferencváros (Hungary)
26	Anderlecht (Belgium)
26	Juventus (Italy)

MOST LEAGUE GAMES IN A COUNTRY		
Austria	Robert Sara	581
Denmark	Aage Rou Jensen	709
Czech Rep.	Libor Janácek	278
England	Peter Shilton	1,005
France	Jean-Luc Ettori	601
Germany	Charly Körbel	602
Greece	Dimitrios Domazos	536
Hungary	Gyorgy Szabo	507
Italy	Dino Zoff	570
Netherlands	Pim Doesburg	687
Scotland	Bob Ferrier	626
Spain	Andoni Zubizarreta	622
Sweden	Thomas Ravelli	430
Turkey	Metin Oktay	698

Winger Francisco Gento **won an astonishing 12 league championships** with Spanish giants Real Madrid in the 1950s and 1960s.

Thierry Henry (left) and Freddie Ljungberg, Arsenal, 2002

Premier League

The **oldest footballer** to play in the English Premier League was John Burridge. In 1995, he played for Manchester City at the age of **43 years and 5 months**. In his long career, Burridge played for 26 different clubs.

Since the Premier League started in 1992, Manchester United have **never finished lower than third**. They have won 15 English championship titles (including English League titles). This puts them second behind Liverpool, who won the English League 18 times, but have never won the Premier League.

Arsenal was the first ⏵ club to **remain unbeaten** in the Premier League all season when they won the 2003/04 championship.

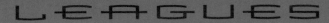
Around the world

Australia unveiled its brand new top league, the A-League, in 2005/06. It features ten teams, including one from another country – the New Zealand Knights.

The Fiji Premier League has an unusual but exciting title – **The Battle of the Giants**!

For three seasons (2001-2003), the Women's United Soccer Association (WUSA) ran the **world's first professional league for women**. Atlanta Beat won more games than any other team – 30 out of their 63 matches – but lost once in the semi-final and twice in the final, so never won the title.

The **world's smallest football league** has only two teams. The Scillonian League (on the Isles of Scilly) features Woolpack Wanderers and Garrison Gunners as they slog it out over a 20 game league season. If that wasn't enough, the sides play each other in two cup competitions as well!

Hungarian footballer Alfred Schaffer won the league championship 16 times with two clubs – Ferencváros and MTK. He played for **an astonishing 21 different clubs** in total.

Step out on to the pitch of English League club Chester City's Deva Stadium and **you are in Wales**. Only the easternmost part of the stadium (housing the club offices) is in England, allowing the club to play in England.

Despite beginning all the way back in 1966, **only three teams have ever won** the 14-team league championship in the African nation of Mali: Djoliba AC, Stade Malien and AS Real.

Trabzonspor won the 1979/80 Turkish league championship, despite only scoring **25 goals in 30 games**.

Two players have won 12 league championships with Portuguese side Benfica – Mario Coluna and Eusebio.

Yo-yo clubs

Some teams are a little too good for one lower division, but not quite good enough for the division above. The result can be a yo-yo, with the team gaining promotion only to be relegated the next season or a couple of seasons later. These teams have yo-yoed the most between the top two divisions of their country's league.

Haladas (Hungary) - 13 promotions, 12 relegations
Leicester City (England) - 11 promotions, 11 relegations
CD Malaga (Spain) - 11 promotions, 11 relegations
Brescia (Italy) - 10 promotions, 11 relegations
Atalanta (Italy) - 10 promotions, 10 relegations
Morton (Scotland) - 10 promotions, 10 relegations

Doubles and trebles

Winning a country's league and its cup competition is known as, '**doing the double**'. Scottish club Rangers have managed to complete the double 17 times – a world record co-held with Linfield of Northern Ireland.

Manchester United and PSV Eindhoven have both won the **highest possible European trebles** – their national league, the main domestic cup and the European Champions Cup. PSV did it in 1988 and Manchester United in 1999.

Promotion and relegation

Four clubs joined the Dutch league when it formed in 1956 and **have yet to experience relegation**: Ajax, Feyenoord, PSV Eindhoven and FC Utrecht.

⬇ In 1999, Kawasaki Frontale became the first team ever to be **promoted from J-League 2 into J-League 1**. The following year, they became the first to be relegated to J-League 2, but 2005 saw them promoted back up into the top division.

Hideaki Kitajima (left) of Kashiwa Reysol and Toshiya Hattori of Jubilo Iwata fighting to stay top of the J-League in 2001

Europe's Golden Boot

Since 1996/97, European Sports Magazines (ESM) have awarded a Golden Boot to the highest goalscorer in leagues in Europe. Goalscorers playing in the top leagues in Europe have their goals counting double. This means that, in some years, the player who scored the most goals did not win the Golden Boot (they are shown in brackets).

1996/97	Ronaldo – FC Barcelona, Spain, 34 goals (Tony Bird – Barry Town, Wales, 42 goals)
1997/98	Nikos Mahlas – Vitesse, Netherlands, 34 goals (Rainer Rauffmann – Omonia, Cyprus, 42 goals)
1998/99	Mário Jardel – FC Porto, Portugal, 36 goals
1999/00	Kevin Phillips – Sunderland, England, 30 goals (Mário Jardel – FC Porto, Portugal, 38 goals)
2000/01	Henrik Larsson – Celtic, Scotland, 35 goals
2001/02	Mário Jardel – Sporting Lisbon, Portugal, 42 goals (Marc Lloyd Williams – Bangor City, Wales, 47 goals)
2002/03	Roy Makaay – RC Deportivo, Spain, 29 goals (Andrei Krölov – Tallina VMK, Estonia, 37 goals)
2003/04	Thierry Henry – Arsenal, England, 30 goals (Ara Hakobian – Banants Yerevan, Armenia, 45 goals)
2004/05	Thierry Henry – Arsenal, England, 25 goals and Diego Forlan – Villareal, Spain, 25 goals

Winning streaks

In 1991/92, AC Milan won 22 and drew 12 of their 34 games to go **unbeaten through a league season**. Egyptian side Al-Ahly did even better in 2004/05, winning 24, drawing two and losing none of their Egyptian league games.

Some clubs have done even better. Celtic managed **a run of 65 league wins** during World War I, Boca Juniors won 59 games in a row in the 1920s and AC Milan went 58 games without losing between 1991 and 1993.

Latvian club Skonto Riga won the league championship in 2004. Few raised their eyebrows – Skonto Riga had **won the 13 previous competitions too**!

Think winning a treble is special? In 1921/22, Linfield FC of Northern Ireland won the league, the Irish Cup, the Intermediate Cup, the County Antrim Shield, the New Charity Cup, the Gold Cup and the City Cup – seven trophies in all!

Dutch club Ajax **had a great 1972**. They won the Dutch League, the Dutch Cup, the European Cup, the Intercontinental Cup and the European Super Cup.

Tunisian side Esperance went unbeaten for 85 league games (1997-2001), while Steaua Bucharest went **a whopping 104 games unbeaten** in the Romanian league (1986-89).

Real Madrid were the world's greatest club side in the late 1950s and early 1960s. Between 1957 and 1965, Real were **not beaten at home for 121 games in a row**.

Everton's Dixie Dean is believed to be the record holder for the most goals scored in a major league in a season. He **netted an amazing 60 goals** in the 1927/28 season.

If you cannot win the league, there's always a chance of success in a cup competition. Every country runs a number of cup competitions for its clubs, and the best teams in a country often play in international cup competitions as well.

Juventus star Gaetano Scirea (2nd right) fighting for possession in the 1983 European Cup quarter-final

The oldest cup of all

The Football Association Challenge Cup began in 1872, and is the oldest surviving cup competition in the world. In 1927, the FA Cup was **won by a non-English side** for the one and only time. Cardiff City from Wales beat Arsenal 1-0.

Lord Kinnaird played in nine FA Cup finals between 1873 and 1882, winning five. He was on the committee of the FA at the age of 22, and was FA president for 33 years. In 1910, Kinnaird was **presented with the old FA Cup trophy to keep**!

Players gathering round injured Manchester City goalkeeper Bert Trautman at the 1956 FA Cup final

Copa Libertadores

There are many cup competitions in South America, but the **biggest club prize of all** is the Copa Libertadores. It has been won most often by Argentinean side Independiente, with seven victories.

Sporting Cristal of Peru holds the record of **17 consecutive matches unbeaten** in the Copa Libertadores.

Uruguyan side Peñarol have competed in more Copas than any other team. They have **won 140 games** and won the Copa five times.

Cup sorcerers

Chelsea lost 13-0 to Caledonia AIA of Trinidad and Tobago in a 1999 cup game. Relax – it was the Chelsea club from the nation of St Vincent and Grenadines in The CONCACAF Cup!

Gaetano Scirea **secured all three of Europe's top club honours** while playing for Juventus – the European Cup, the Cup Winners' Cup and the UEFA Cup.

Selangor have won the Malaysian Cup a **record 31 times** since it was first played in 1921.

Champions League

For clubs in Europe, **this is the big one.** It began in 1956 as the European Champions Cup, and became the Champions League in 1992/93. In the thrilling 2005 final, Liverpool won on penalties to claim the Cup for the fifth time, which means they keep it.

Real Madrid have **won the competition a record nine times**, and that includes the first five European Cups in a row.

Alfredo di Stefano held the record for **most goals scored** in the European Cup (49) until Spain's Raúl equalled his total in 2004. Both played for Real Madrid.

UEFA and Cup-Winners Cups ⚽

Belgian side FC Brugges qualified for and played in the UEFA Cup for **nine seasons in a row**, including the 2004/05 season.

Two teams have entered the European Cup-Winners' Cup **five years in a row**: Reipas Lahti of Finland and Welsh club Cardiff City.

In 1984/85, QPR thought they had Partizan Belgrade on the ropes after winning their first UEFA Cup leg 6-2. Unfortunately, they lost the return match 4-0 and **went out on away goals**!

CSKA Moscow's Vagner Love scoring the third goal in the 2005 UEFA Cup final against Sporting Lisbon

⏶ CSKA Moscow became the **first Russian team to win a major European Cup competition** when they beat Sporting Lisbon to win the 2004/05 UEFA Cup.

Five teams have won the Cup-Winners' Cup **without winning their own cup competition**! They are Fiorentina (1961), Rangers (1972), Anderlecht (1978), Dinamo Tblisi (1981) and Barcelona (1991).

One of the **biggest mismatches in UEFA Cup history** occurred in 1972, when Dutch side Feyenoord beat US Rumelange of Luxembourg 9-0. Feyenoord then won the second game 12-0 to win 21-0 overall.

EUROPEAN CHAMPIONS CUP AND CHAMPIONS LEAGUE WINNERS

1956	Real Madrid
1957	Real Madrid
1958	Real Madrid
1959	Real Madrid
1960	Real Madrid
1961	Benfica
1962	Benfica
1963	AC Milan
1964	Inter Milan
1965	Inter Milan
1966	Real Madrid
1967	Celtic
1968	Manchester United
1969	AC Milan
1970	Feyenoord
1971	Ajax
1972	Ajax
1973	Ajax
1974	Bayern Munich
1975	Bayern Munich
1976	Bayern Munich
1977	Liverpool
1978	Liverpool
1979	Nottingham Forest
1980	Nottingham Forest
1981	Liverpool
1982	Aston Villa
1983	SV Hamburg
1984	Liverpool
1985	Juventus
1986	Steaua Bucharest
1987	Porto
1988	PSV Eindhoven
1989	AC Milan
1990	AC Milan
1991	Red Star Belgrade
1992	Barcelona
1993	Marseilles
1994	AC Milan
1995	Ajax
1996	Juventus
1997	Borussia Dortmund
1998	Real Madrid
1999	Manchester United
2000	Real Madrid
2001	Bayern Munich
2002	Real Madrid
2003	AC Milan
2004	Porto
2005	Liverpool

In 1899, the English FA suggested to its clubs that there should be a maximum £10 limit on footballer transfer fees. But, 102 years later, French star Zinedine Zidane moved from Juventus to Real Madrid for a world record fee of £45.6 million! Football today is big business, with top clubs being run as major companies.

Real Madrid's expensive all-star line-up (left to right): Esteban Cambiasso, Zinedine Zidane, Luis Figo, Ronaldo and David Beckham

Mega money

When Everton won the English First Division in 1963, after splashing out £100,000 on players in 1962, they were referred to as '**the cheque-book champions**'. Fast forward to 2004/05, and the Chelsea squad that lifted the Premier League title. The club's owner, Roman Abramovich, had spent more than £200 million on players alone.

The small Italian village of Peschici won approximately £23 million on the national lottery in 1998. They immediately **put in a bid for Brazilian legend Ronaldo** to play for their village side!

Freddy Adu in training for the USA team, 2004

Inter Milan offered about £500,000 for Freddy Adu back in 2000. His family turned it down. After all, Freddy **was only ten years of age**!

Out of pocket

In 1993, the Albanian FA refused to let its players swap shirts with the Spanish team after an international game – they **couldn't afford replacement shirts**.

In 2005, Dinel Staicu, owner of Romanian club Universitatea Craiova, offered the club to the local council **for free**. He later considered auctioning It on Ebay!

In 2002, Danish Superleague side Lyngby FC **declared itself bankrupt**. They played the rest of that season, but then dropped two divisions and reformed as amateur club Lyngby BK.

2004 TOP 10 WORLD MANAGER ANNUAL EARNINGS (£MILLIONS)		
José Mourinho	5.1	Chelsea
Sir Alex Ferguson	4.1	Manchester United
Sven-Göran Eriksson	4.0	England (national team)
Arsène Wenger	3.0	Arsenal
Ottmar Hitzfeld	2.3	Bayern Munich
Fabio Capello	2.2	Juventus
Jürgen Klinsmann	2.1	Germany (national team)
Claudio Ranieri	2.0	Valencia CF
Rafael Benitez	1.8	Liverpool
Alberto Zaccheroni	1.6	Internazionale

2004 TOP 10 WORLD FOOTBALLER ANNUAL EARNINGS (£MILLIONS)		
David Beckham	19.8	Real Madrid
Ronaldo	13.4	Real Madrid
Zinedine Zidane	8.9	Real Madrid
Christian Vieri	8.2	Internazionale
Alessandro del Piero	6.5	Juventus
Frank Lampard	6.4	Chelsea
Raúl	6.3	Real Madrid
Thierry Henry	6.3	Arsenal
John Terry	5.9	Chelsea
Luis Figo	5.8	Real Madrid

Transfer fee free

A handful of players are transferred for tens of millions of pounds, but **many players are sold for far less**, move on free transfers or are swapped for the strangest things.

Daniel Allende was signed by Uruguyan side Central Espanol from Rentistas in 1979 for **550 beef steaks**, to be supplied at a rate of 25 a week!

Manchester United hold the UK transfer record, paying £30 million in 2002 for Rio Ferdinand. But, back in 1927, their swoop for midfielder Hughie McLenahan cost them just **three freezers full of ice-cream**.

Tony Cascarino (right) playing for Ireland against Turkey's Ozalan Alpay, 1999

Tony Cascarino was transferred from Crockenhill FC to Gillingham in 1982 in exchange for some **iron panels to repair the stadium and a new strip** – an estimated fee of £180. The big striker went on to play for Aston Villa and Marseilles and become the Republic of Ireland's third most capped player, with 88 appearances.

TOP TRANSFER FEES UP TO SEPTEMBER 2005 (£MILLIONS)

£45.6 – Zinedine Zidane, Juventus to Real Madrid (2001)
£37 – Luis Figo, Barcelona to Real Madrid (2000)
£35.5 – Hernan Crespo, Parma to Lazio (2000)
£32.6 – Gianluigi Buffon, Parma to Juventus (2001)
£32 – Christian Vieri, Lazio to Inter Milan (1999)

TOP 10 RICHEST CLUBS BY INCOME IN 2003/04 SEASON

1	Manchester United	£171.5m
2	Real Madrid	£156.3m
3	AC Milan	£147.2m
4	Chelsea	£143.7m
5	Juventus	£142.4m
6	Arsenal	£115m
7	Barcelona	£110.1m
8	Inter Milan	£110.3m
9	Bayern Munich	£110.1m
10	Liverpool	£92.3m

Christian Vieri (left) playing for Lazio in 1999, before his transfer to Inter Milan

Stadiums (**stadia**) **are where** the big games are held. Some grounds like the Maracaná in Brazil, the San Siro in Italy and the Nou Camp in Spain are incredibly famous. New stadiums cost a lot of money to build. Old Trafford, where Manchester United play, cost £60,000 to complete in 1910. The final cost of the new Wembley Stadium is expected to be £757 million!

English Conference North team Northwich Victoria's Drill Field is believed to be the **oldest surviving football ground** still in use. It was completed in 1874.

Azerbaijan's national stadium is named after the linesman, Tofik Bakhramov, who famously awarded the **controversial third goal** in the 1966 World Cup final to England.

Austrian side Sturm Graz play their home games at the Arnold Schwarzenegger stadium, **named after the movie star**.

White Hart Lane is the home of Tottenham Hotspur. But, during World War I, it was turned into a **gas mask-making factory**!

Highs and lows

Germany's Borussia Dortmund boast the highest attendance of any club. During the 2004/05 season, they averaged **77,353 spectators** every league game. Local rivals Schalke had an average of 61,241.

The **highest attendance** at a World Cup game was 199,850 in 1950 at the Maracaná Stadium in Brazil.

The lowest attendance for an English league game occurred in 1921 and featured Stockport County playing Leicester City. Just **13 people turned up**.

The lowest attendance for a World Cup Finals game was in 1930. Romania beat Peru 3-1, and just **300 or so spectators** watched the match.

Borussia Dortmund fans at the 2002 UEFA Cup final

Mexico v Japan was the game that **broke Olympic football records**, with 105,000 fans crammed into Mexico's Azteca stadium.

120,000 fans watched the Morocco v Cameroon World Cup qualifier in 1981.

Brazil's enormous Macaraná stadium in Rio de Janeiro

THE WORLD'S BIGGEST STADIUMS BY COUNTRY		
Argentina	El Monumental	70,645
Brazil	Maracaná	103,022
England	Wembley	90,000
France	Stade de France	79,959
Germany	Westfalenstadion	82,700
Italy	Giuseppe Meazza (San Siro)	85,700
Japan	Yokohama	72,370
Mexico	Azteca	105,064
Portugal	Da Luz	65,647
Russia	Olimpiyskiv	84,745
Spain	Camp Nou	98,934
Ukraine	NSK	83,450
USA	Giants Stadium	80,242
Wales	Millennium Stadium	73,500

The English FA **banned the use of floodlights** in 1930 – a ban that stayed in force until the 1950s.

During the 1995/96 season, English club Blackpool **fitted a heated bench** for their substitutes to sit on during cold winter matches. The visiting team, however, got a hard and cold wooden bench!

The first World Cup qualifying match to be played on an **artificial pitch** was in 1976, when Canada and the USA played in Vancouver.

Stadium features

Aberdeen's Pittodrie stadium became the **first all-seater football ground in Britain** in 1880. A year later, Coventry City's Highfield Road became the first all-seater football ground in England.

The first-ever Brazilian floodlight match was played on 23 June, 1923 between AA Republica and SE Linhas e Cabos. The **pitch was illuminated with the headlights of trams**. The first Brazilian stadium with real floodlights was Vasco da Gama's ground, in 1928.

Carlisle United's Brunton Park pitch under flood water in 2005

Weather wonders

During the 1973/74 season, Scottish clubs Inverness Thistle and Falkirk **tried to play their match a staggering 30 times**. The first 29 were postponed due to bad weather. When they finally met, Falkirk won 4-0.

Grenada's 2004 Premier League season was **abandoned due to Hurricane Ivan**.

In 1945, Arsenal were playing Russian giants Dynamo Moscow in London when **a thick fog descended over the ground**. The referee refused to abandon the game as the visitors had come such a long way, but it was impossible to see what was going on. It is said that an Arsenal player who was sent off sneaked back on, while the Soviet side may have brought on substitutes to boost their numbers to 12 or 13. Dynamo Moscow won 3-2.

The very first international match took place in 1873 – England and Scotland fought out a 0-0 'snore' draw! There have been hundreds of more exciting and fascinating international games since.

Chelsea star Eider Gudjohnsen was brought on as a 62nd minute substitute when Iceland were playing Estonia in 1996. **The man he replaced? His father, Arnor!** That was the closest the dad and his lad ever got to playing alongside each other for their country.

India used to insist on playing their international matches without football boots and in **bare feet**. FIFA wouldn't let them do this at the 1950 World Cup, so they **didn't turn up**!

Former Brazilian international Socrates playing for English side Garforth Town, aged 50

Caps stats

Appearing for your country's full national team is known as getting a cap. **It is a great honour.** Some of the very best footballers reach a century of caps (100). In 2004, Karel Poborsky became the first Czech Republic player to appear for his country 100 times.

In 1976, Bobby Moore played with Brazilian legend Pelé in a US team against England. The match **celebrated America's 200 years of independence**.

A few players have been **capped by more than one country**. Davor Suker played for Yugoslavia twice and Croatia 69 times. Lubomir Moravcik won 42 caps for Czechoslovakia and 38 for Slovakia.

Kristine Lilly is the **most capped player in the world**. She has represented the USA women's team 282 times.

The Netherlands' brothers Frank and Ronald de Boer have **179 caps between them**.

Another **pair of brothers** have even more caps. Egypt's Ibrahim Hassam has a fantastic 125 caps for his country. His brother, Hossam, has 163!

Pelé and Bobby Moore teaming up against England in 1976

Longest unbeaten runs in international football		
31	Argentina	Feb 1991-Aug 1993
30	Hungary	June 1950-July 1954
29	Brazil	March 1970-June 1973
27	Brazil	Dec 1993-July 1995
27	France	Feb 1994-June 1996

International goals

Ali Daei has **played an impressive 142 times for Iran**, and has scored four or more goals in a single game five times!

International strikers who score more than one goal every two games are rated as top notch. Just Fontaine averaged three goals every two games, **scoring 30 times** in 20 matches.

The **fastest hat-trick** in international football was scored by England player Willie Hall in 1938 against Ireland. He scored three times in three and a half minutes!

Lothar Matthäus playing for Germany against Portugal in Euro 2000

Most international appearances

CAPS	PLAYER	COUNTRY
173	Mohamed Al-Deayea	Saudi Arabia
172	Claudio Suárez	Mexico
164	Cobi Jones	USA
164	Adnan Khamees Al-Talyani	UAE
163	Hossam Hassan	Egypt
150	Sami Al-Jaber	Saudi Arabia
150	Lothar Matthäus	West Germany, Germany
143	Mohammed Al-Khilaiwi	Saudi Arabia
143	Marko Kristal	Estonia
143	Thomas Ravelli	Sweden
142	Ali Daei	Iran
141	Martin Reim	Estonia
139	Majed Abdullah	Saudi Arabia
135	Myung-Bo Hong	South Korea
134	Jeff Agoos	USA
132	Cafu	Brazil
130	Jorge Campos	Mexico
129	Peter Schmeichel	Denmark
128	Marcelo Balboa	USA
126	Paolo Maldini	Italy
126	Andoni Zubizarreta	Spain

Disability no barrier

Hungarian keeper Karoly Zsak had a **finger amputated** after an accident, but won 30 caps playing in goal for his country.

Héctor Castro played for Uruguay, despite **losing his right hand** in a woodwork accident before the 1930 World Cup. He scored Uruguay's fourth goal in the final as Uruguay beat Argentina 4-2.

Garrincha was an international star for Brazil, and player of the tournament at the 1962 World Cup. But he was **crippled by polio** as a child, which left him with his left leg bent inwards and his right leg 6cm shorter than his left.

Not an international yet, but one to watch, is Kenya's Fred Ogallo. Now playing for Kenyan Premier League side, Mathare United, Ogallo is **completely deaf** and cannot speak well. He has overcome his disabilities to play senior football in his country.

The **European Championships** is second only to the World Cup as a major international football competition. Qualifying is almost as intense as for the World Cup. All teams are desperate to win the Henri Delaunay trophy, named after the Frenchman who helped found UEFA and the Euro Champs competition.

The fastest goal ever scored at the Euro Finals was by Dmitri Kirichenko, who **scored in 67 seconds** for Russia against Greece.

Euro 2000 was the first tournament to have **two host nations** – Belgium and the Netherlands. The 2008 competition will also be co-hosted – by Alpine neighbours Austria and Switzerland.

England, the Netherlands and Germany are the three teams who have **successfully qualified for the last five European Championships** (1988-2004). England are the only side of the three never to have won the competition.

The women's Euro Champs

The very first women's European Championships took place between 1982 and 1984. Instead of playing a one match final, the two sides played two matches, one home and one away.

At Euro 2005, England suffered a **1-0 loss to Sweden** in the quarter-final. At the first European Champs, they lost to Sweden on penalties in the final and at the next they lost at the semi-final stage, again to Sweden!

Birgit Prinz **broke the German goalscoring record** at Euro 2005, scoring her 84th goal as Germany thrashed France 4-0 in the group stages.

Hanna Ljungberg, a star striker for Sweden at Euro 2005, was at the centre of an **amazing transfer attempt** in 2003. Luciano Gaucci, president of Italian Serie A men's side, Perugia, tried to sign her!

Jürgen Klinsmann of Germany battling for the ball with Jan Suchoparek of the Czech Republic during the Euro 96 final

46

WOMEN'S EUROPEAN CHAMPIONSHIP			
WINNERS	SCORE		RUNNERS-UP
1982/84	Sweden	4-3 (pens)	England
1984/86	Norway	2-1	Sweden
1987/89	West Germany	4-1	Norway
1989/91	West Germany	3-1	Norway
1991/93	Norway	1-0	Italy
1993/95	Germany	3-2	Sweden
1995/97	Germany	2-0	Italy
1999/01	Germany	1-0	Sweden
2005	Germany	3-1	Finland

EUROPEAN CHAMPIONSHIP FINALS	
1960	USSR 2-1 Yugoslavia
1964	Spain 2-1 USSR
1968	Italy 2-0 Yugoslavia (after replay)
1972	West Germany 3-0 USSR
1976	Czechoslovakia 2-2 West Germany (5-3 pens)
1980	West Germany 2-1 Belgium
1984	France 2-0 Spain
1988	Netherlands 2-0 USSR
1992	Denmark 2-0 Germany
1996	Germany 2-1 Czech Republic
2000	France 2-1 Italy
2004	Greece 1-0 Portugal

Against the odds

Greece were **rank outsiders** to win Euro 2004, only tiny Latvia had longer odds. But the Greek team beat hosts Portugal, not only in the first game of the competition but also in the final to win their first major competition.

Maniche of Portugal in the Euro 2004 final

Denmark manager, Richard Moller Nielsen, was at home **decorating his kitchen** after his side failed to qualify for Euro 92. He heard that Yugoslavia had withdrawn and his side were replacements – with only two weeks to go!

Luxembourg had its most **glorious and heartbreaking** footballing moments back in 1963. They beat Holland 3-2 to make the quarter-finals of the 1964 competition. They then drew with Denmark 2-2 and 3-3, but lost out on reaching the semi-final on away goals.

Big winners

Two teams, Germany and the Netherlands, have won the most Euro Champs Finals games – 15. Germany (together with West Germany) holds the record for the **most Euro Champs final appearances**, five in total.

Croatian striker Davor Suker has the record for the **most goals** scored in one competition, including qualifying and Finals. He scored 15 goals in Euro 96.

The tiny principality of Luxembourg holds **two unwanted records** – the most defeats in all Euro Champs matches (65) and the most goals let in (232).

French striker Michel Platini **scored nine goals** at Euro 1984, a record for the Finals.

Weird and wonderful

France's David Trezeguet scoring the winning goal of the Euro 2000 final

During Euro 2000, football fan Raymond Brul was faced with a problem. He had a Dutch mother and a Belgian father. To show support for both sides, **he painted his car** half in Belgian colours and half in Dutch!

Two Englishmen from Bristol **locked themselves in a shed** with a TV to watch the whole of Euro 2000.

In the weekend before Euro 2004, the Bulgarian team **stopped training** to go to the wedding of their striker, Vladimir Manchev.

During Euro 2004, the English FA ordered **24 bottles of hairstyling mousse** for the players of the England team!

There are many other major international competitions as well as the World Cup. Football is played on every continent, and there is at least one continental competition for national teams of each one.

Copa America

The South American Copa America competition kicked off in 1910, making it the **oldest surviving international competition**. It featured three teams: Argentina (the winners), Chile and Uruguay.

Uruguay has a fantastic record in the Copa America. In 38 matches, it has **never been beaten at home**!

Brazil won its first Copa in 1919 and its last in 1999. It has a total of six wins in all. The 1919 final between Brazil and Uruguay **lasted 150 minutes**, with 90 of regular time and two 30-minute extra-time periods. Phew!

Countries with the **most wins** in the Copa are Argentina with 15 and Uruguay with 14.

Diego Forlan of Uruguay playing in the 2004 Copa America

African Cup of Nations

The very first African Cup of Nations took place in 1957, and **only three teams entered**. In 2002, 50 nations competed in qualifying for the 16 places in the Finals.

The Ivory Coast's Alain Gouamene has **competed in seven** different African Nations Cups, the last in 2000.

In senior football, you have to have at least seven players on the pitch or the game will be abandoned. In the African Cup of Nations qualifying campaign in 2003, a match between Cape Verde and Mauritania had to be abandoned after **five Mauritanian players were sent off**.

Countries with the **most wins** in the African Cup of Nations are Egypt, Ghana and Cameroon (four each).

Men's Olympic Games

	GOLD	SILVER	BRONZE
1908	United Kingdom	Denmark	Netherlands
1912	United Kingdom	Denmark	Netherlands
1920	Belgium	Spain	Netherlands
1924	Uruguay	Switzerland	Sweden
1928	Uruguay	Argentina	Italy
1936	Italy	Austria	Norway
1948	Sweden	Yugoslavia	Denmark
1952	Hungary	Yugoslavia	Sweden
1956	Soviet Union	Yugoslavia	Bulgaria
1960	Yugoslavia	Denmark	Netherlands
1964	Hungary	Czechoslovakia	East Germany
1968	Hungary	Bulgaria	Japan
1972	Poland	Hungary	East Germany/ Soviet Union
1976	East Germany	Poland	Soviet Union
1980	Czechoslovakia	East Germany	Soviet Union
1984	France	Brazil	Yugoslavia
1988	Soviet Union	Brazil	West Germany
1992	Spain	Poland	Ghana
1996	Nigeria	Argentina	Brazil
2000	Cameroon	Spain	Chile
2004	Argentina	Paraguay	Italy

Olympic Games

Until the arrival of the FIFA World Cup, **the Olympics was considered football's world championship**. One of the reasons why the first World Cup was hosted in Uruguay was because it won the Olympics in 1928.

Idriss Carlos Kameni was **just 16 years of age** when he played in goal for Cameroon in the 2000 Olympic final. He proved himself a hero as early as the fifth minute, when he saved a Spanish penalty. Cameroon won the tournament. ▶

Carlos Kameni, Cameroon

At the 2000 Olympics, Cameroon's Jean-Paul Akono became the **first African** to coach a team to win a major world soccer competition.

Japan has **never won** the Olympics, but its teams have scored more goals in qualifying and Finals tournaments than any other team – 283.

Poor Sri Lanka. Its teams have played a total of 20 Olympic qualifying matches. They **lost all 20** matches, scored 7 goals and **let in 100 goals**!

Asia and Oceania

Hiroshi Nanami, Japan

 Three nations have won the Asian Nations Cup **three times**: Japan in 1992, 2000 and 2004; Saudi Arabia in 1984, 1988 and 1996; Iran in 1968, 1972 and 1976.

The **2007 Asian Nations Cup** is going to be hosted by not one, two or three different countries, but by four: Indonesia, Malaysia, Thailand and Vietnam.

Oceania's two biggest countries, Australia and New Zealand, dominate football in Oceania, but some of the smaller island nations have had their day. **Tahiti was runner-up** in the first, second and third Oceania Nations Cup.

In 21 Oceania Nations Cup matches between 1973 and 2002, Australia has scored **110 goals**, letting in only nine.

There were no referees when football first started. Instead, each team nominated an umpire to enforce rules and settle disputes. Referees were put in charge in 1891, and the two umpires became the referee's assistants. The fourth assistant – the person who holds up the board showing extra-time – arrived on the scene exactly 100 years after the first refs.

Fourth assistant
Felipe Ramos Rizo

Referees **have to be very fit**. According to FIFA, a typical referee will travel over 11.2km in a match.

Tesfaye Gebreyesus from Eritrea has an incredible ref's record. He refereed at **six African Nations Cups** – from 1970 to 1986.

By 2004, Danish referee Kim Milton Nielsen had refereed 134 international matches and 44 Champions League games, making him **the most experienced top level referee** around.

In 2003, the Norwegian postal service put a **referee's face on a stamp**. The only trouble was that the image wasn't Norwegian ref Lars Johan Hammer as planned, but Peter Hertel – a German lower-league referee.

Most games refereed at World Cups
8 Joël Quiniou (France) 1986-1994
7 Jan Langenus (Belgium) 1930-1938
7 Benjamin Griffiths (Wales) 1950-1958
7 Juan Gardeazábal (Spain) 1958-1966
7 Ali Bujsaim (United Arab Emirates) 1994-2002

Whistle stop

Before the days of refs with whistles, football umpires **waved a handkerchief** to signal a foul or stoppage.

The most famous make of referee's whistle is the **Acme Thunderer**, first made in 1860 by British toolmaker, Joseph Hudson. The company Hudson & Co. has produced more than 160 million whistles.

In a non-league match in Manchester, England, between St Cass and Pinewood, the referee **forgot to bring a whistle** and ended up using a mouth organ instead!

World Cup refs

Nicole Petignat keeping AIK's Krister Nordin under control

⚫ Nicole Petignat is a referee in the Austrian and Swiss men's leagues. She officiated at the 1999 Women's World Cup final and, in August 2003, she became the **first female referee** for a men's UEFA Cup game – the AIK Solna versus Fylkir match.

Ulises Saucedo was a referee at the 1930 World Cup. **He was also the coach** of South American side Bolivia, but didn't referee their games.

A referee at the 1962 World Cup had a great name – **Edward Charles Faultless**!

The referee in the 2002 ▶ World Cup final was Pierluigi Collina, **football's most famous referee**. He now has to retire from Italy's Serie A because the maximum age is 45.

Pierluigi Collina

Losing it

In Chimbote, Peru, in 1974, **the referee came to blows with his assistant**! Alipio Montejo and Gonzalo Morote argued over whether or not a goal should stand. They then started fighting and the players had to separate them!

English referee Martin Sylvester **sent himself off** in an Andover and District Sunday League match in 1998. He had lost his temper and punched a player.

In 2001, a Champions League game between Austrian side Tirol Innsbruck and Russia's Lokomotiv Moscow had to be replayed due to a refereeing error. The ref gave Lokomotiv player Rousian Pimenov two yellow cards, but **forgot to send him off**!

In 2002, Belgian referee Marc Gevaert decided to end a game between FC Wiftschate and Vladslo early. **He felt sorry for Wiftschate**, who were losing 16-0.

In 2001, Wimpole 2000 were losing 18-1 to Earls Colne Reserves in the Great Bromley Cup in England, when the referee, Brian Savill, **volleyed the ball into the net** to make the score 18-2. The authorities banned him for seven weeks.

No one was sent off at the 1950 and 1970 World Cups, but **22 red cards** were handed out in 1998.

51

Thousands of games were played before penalties were invented. The first penalty given was actually a mistake! A ref awarded it to Scottish club Airdrieonians in 1891 – but the new penalty rule was not supposed to be used until the start of the next season.

Ruud Van Nistelrooy scores a penalty for Manchester United

Johan Cruyff scored an outrageous penalty for Dutch club Ajax against Helmond Sport in 1982. He **tricked the keeper** into diving, and rolled the ball forward and to the side for team-mate Jesper Olsen. Olsen returned the ball and Cruyff rolled it into the **unprotected goal**.

Legendary Soviet Union goalkeeper, Lev Yashin, is alleged to have **saved more than 150 penalties** throughout his long career.

Did you know that a penalty can travel at **100km/h**, and take just four tenths of a second to reach the goal line?

Southampton and England striker Matthew Le Tissier was a great penalty taker. He missed only one of 50 penalty attempts in his career. He retired in 2002.

Shootouts

In certain matches, a penalty shootout is used to decide a winner when the two teams are **tied after extra-time**.

The first penalty shootout occurred in 1970 in the English Watney Mann Cup between lowly Hull City and Manchester United. Hull lost the shootout 4-3, but Manchester United's Denis Law became **the first person to miss a shootout penalty** along the way.

Did you know that the winners of **two different FIFA World Cups** have been decided by penalty shootouts, and both were in the same stadium? In 1994, Italy lost to Brazil in a penalty shootout while, five years later, the USA women's team beat China on penalties. Both matches were played in the Rose Bowl, California, USA.

The England team were knocked out of Euro 2004 by **a goal from a goalkeeper**! Portuguese keeper Ricardo scored the winning penalty that marked England's fourth loss in five penalty shootout attempts.

Magnus Kihlstedt making a save for Dutch side FC Copenhagen in a penalty shootout during the 2003 UEFA Cup

Most penalties in a shootout

Total	Score	Teams	Competition
48	17-16	KK Palace v Civics	Namibian Cup 2005
44	20-19	Argentinos Juniors v Racing Club	Argentinean League 1988
40	15-15	Obernai v ASCA Wittelsheim	Coupe de France 1996
34	17-16	Gençlerbirligi SK v Galatasaray	SK Turkish Cup 1996

Copa America penalty shootouts

			Result	Penalties
1993	QF	Colombia v Uruguay	1-1	5-3
1993	QF	Argentina v Brazil	1-1	6-5
1993	SF	Argentina v Colombia	0-0	6-5
1995	QF	Colombia v Paraguay	1-1	5-4
1995	QF	Brazil v Argentina	2-2	4-2
1995	QF	United States v Mexico	0-0	4-1
1995	F	Uruguay v Brazil	0-0	5-3
1997	QF	Mexico v Ecuador	1-1	4-3
1999	QF	Mexico v Peru	3-3	4-2
1999	QF	Uruguay v Paraguay	1-1	5-3
1999	QF	Uruguay v Chile	1-1	5-3
2001	3/4 PO	Honduras v Uruguay	2-2	5-4
2004	SF	Brazil v Uruguay	1-1	5-3
2004	F	Brazil v Argentina	2-2	4-2

You can fail to score from a penalty by hitting the woodwork, missing altogether or if the keeper saves it. Martin Palermo of Argentina **missed three penalties** in 1999: the first hit the bar, the second missed and the third was saved!

World Cup penalty shootouts

		Result	Penalties
1982	West Germany v France	3-3	5-4
1986	West Germany v Mexico	0-0	4-1
1986	France v Brazil	1-1	4-3
1986	Belgium v Spain	1-1	5-4
1990	Rep. Ireland v Romania	0-0	5-4
1990	Argentina v Yugoslavia	0-0	3-2
1990	Argentina v Italy	1-1	4-3
1990	West Germany v England	1-1	4-3
1994	Bulgaria v Mexico	1-1	3-1
1994	Sweden v Romania	2-2	5-4
1994	Brazil v Italy	0-0	3-2
1998	Argentina v England	2-2	4-3
1998	France v Italy	0-0	4-3
1998	Brazil v Netherlands	1-1	4-2
2002	Spain v Rep. Ireland	1-1	3-2
2002	South Korea v Spain	0-0	5-3

In the past, **keepers facing a penalty were not allowed to move** before the ball was kicked. If they did move, and saved the penalty, the referee could insist on the penalty being retaken. In a Scottish 1945 game between Kilmarnock and Partick Thistle, Tommy White had to **take a penalty seven times**!

Dan Petrescu of Romania after missing a penalty in the shootout against Sweden in the 1994 World Cup

When a referee shows a player a yellow card, it is a caution or 'booking' for bad conduct. Two yellow cards or a straight red card and the player is sent off. Players have been sent off for decades, but red and yellow cards were not invented until 1966.

Some referees use cards more than others. In the 2003/04 Spanish top division, referee Megia Dávila produced **140 yellow cards** and **15 red cards** in just 18 games!

Argentine striker **Mario Kempes** never had a red or yellow card in his 43-game international career. He retired in 1996. English star **Sir Stanley Matthews** had the same success in 700 league games. He retired in 1965.

In the Germany versus Cameroon match at the 2002 World Cup, Spanish referee Antonio Jesús López Nieto handed out a **total of 16 yellow cards** – a World Cup record!

🔻 Sir Alex Ferguson, **Manchester United's manager**, was sent off by Uriah Rennie during a match between United and Newcastle in 2003.

Cameroon's Rigobert Song achieved the unenviable feat of becoming the **only player** to have been sent off at a World Cup **more than once**. He was sent off against Brazil in 1994 and then against Chile in 1998.

Referee Uriah Rennie

Ken Aston refereeing schoolboys in 1962

🔺 Red and yellow cards were invented by English referee Ken Aston. He was driving and thinking how to communicate a caution or sending off to players who do not speak English, when he was **inspired by a set of traffic lights**. The cards were in place in time for the 1970 World Cup.

Cheats!

Some people in football have simply cheated to gain an advantage or to take revenge. Douglas Park, a director of Scottish professional club Hearts, was fined £1,000 in 1988 after **locking referee David Symes in a changing room** for 20 minutes after a match.

Chile were losing a World Cup qualifying game against Brazil in 1989, when their keeper Roberto Rojas **pretended he had been injured** by a firecracker thrown on to the pitch. He pulled out a razor blade hidden in his glove and cut himself. The game was abandoned as he hoped, but video evidence showed he had cheated, and he received a life ban. Chile were also banned from entering the 1994 World Cup.

In a 2004 Italian Serie B game between Avellino and Atalanta, Avellino were awarded a penalty. Atalanta's Carmine Gautieri cheated by **wiping out the penalty spot**. It took six minutes for a steward to come on and re-paint the spot. The penalty taker Marco Capparella had to wait, and **when he finally took his kick he missed**!

Referee Joel Quiniou showing José Batista (sitting on the ground) a red card

Speedy sendings off

In 1992, Chelsea player Vinnie Jones fouled Sheffield United's Dane Whitehouse and received a yellow card **just three seconds after kick-off** – a British, and possibly world, record.

The second-fastest booking in British football was given five seconds into a match. It was also in 1992 and it was also Vinnie Jones who received it! Jones received **13 red cards** in his professional career before he went on to become a film actor.

Bologna's Giuseppe Lorenzo was sent off **after just 10 seconds** in an Italian league match against Parma in 1990 for striking an opponent.

Jamaican international Walter Boyd was about to come on as a substitute for Swansea in the 2000/01 season, when he **hit an opponent**. He was sent off after zero seconds on the pitch!

🔻 1986 saw the fastest ever sending off at a World Cup. Uruguay's José Batista was given a red card for a **bad foul** on Scotland's Gordon Strachan after only 56 seconds of the game!

BRITISH FOOTBALL

Football began in England and Scotland before spreading throughout the world. The British game is chock-full of records and amazing facts. Here's a good one – the shortest game on record was Wolverhampton Wanderers v Stoke in a blizzard in 1894. Only 400 fans turned out and the referee called the match off after just three minutes!

Most international appearances (caps)

ENGLAND		SCOTLAND	
125	Peter Shilton (1970-1990)	102	Kenny Dalglish (1972-1987)
108	Bobby Moore (1962-1973)	91	Jim Leighton (1983-1999)
106	Bobby Charlton (1958-1970)	77	Alex McLeish (1980-1993)
105	Billy Wright (1946-1959)	76	Paul McStay (1984-1997)
90	Bryan Robson (1980-1991)	72	Tommy Boyd (1991-2001)
NORTHERN IRELAND		**WALES**	
119	Pat Jennings (1964-1986)	92	Neville Southall (1982-1998)

Kevin Pressman holds the record for the **fastest sending off** in British professional football – 13 seconds.

In 1984, a game was postponed when a 40-year-old **World War II bomb** was discovered right near Sheffield United's Bramall Lane ground.

20 teams have **won the FA Cup once**. These include two teams you may not be familiar with: Old Carthusians (1881 winners) and Clapham Rovers (1880 winners). Wimbledon – the only team in recent years to move towns and change name (from Milton Keynes Dons) – won in 1988.

West Bromwich Albion fans have an unusual way of supporting their club. They bounce up and down chanting, "**Boing Boing Baggies**". Maybe it's because WBA began life as the Salters Spring Works side?

In 1970, Celtic v Leeds United attracted a **record European Cup attendance** of 135,826.

Celebrity chef Gordon Ramsey was on Oxford United then Glasgow Rangers' books as a teenager. He gave up his professional footballing dreams when he was 18.

Goalkeepers often have longer careers than other footballers. This was certainly the case with England's Peter Shilton, who **played in 1,005 English league games**. He also played 125 times for England.

Dixie Dean holds the record for **the most hat tricks in British football** – 37.

Managers and national teams

England manager Walter Winterbottom holds the record for the **most games in charge of the national team**. He was in charge for 139 games of which 78 were won, 33 drawn and 28 lost.

England manager Sven Goran Eriksson is famous for **making lots of substitutions in friendly matches**. In a game against Australia in 2003, he made an incredible 11 substitutions!

The England manager with the **shortest run in charge** was Peter Taylor. He managed the national side for one game in 2000.

With **70 games** under his belt, Craig Brown has been in charge more times than any other Scottish manager.

At 1.98m (6ft 7in) tall, Peter Crouch became the **tallest player** to play for England when he appeared against the USA in 2005.

In the friendly against Serbia and Montenegro in June 2003, England was **captained by four different players** throughout the match: Michael Owen, Jamie Carragher, Emile Heskey and Phil Neville.

England's **first ever substitution** was in 1950. The great Newcastle United player Jackie Milburn was taken off and Jimmy Mullen of Wolverhampton Wanderers came on. Unlike many substitutes since, **Mullen scored**!

Internationals

Bryan Robson scored the **fastest ever England goal** during the 1982 World Cup Finals in Bilbao. He netted the ball **after just 27 seconds** versus France.

Alan Mullery became the **first England player to be sent off** on 5 June, 1968. By a quirk of fate, the same date in 1999 was the day on which Paul Scholes became the first England player to be sent off on English soil, during a Euro Champs qualifier against Sweden.

While training before the 1958 World Cup Finals, Wales **were told not to play football** in London's Hyde Park by a park keeper, so they had to stop!

Billy Wright and Bobby Moore were England's **longest serving captains**, with 90 caps each as skipper. Wales' largest win was an 11-0 thumping of Ireland back in 1878. Both Scotland and Northern Ireland's **biggest wins** (9-0 and 7-0 respectively) have been over Wales.

MOST ENGLISH LEAGUE WINS (1888/89-2004/05)

18	Liverpool
15	Manchester United
13	Arsenal
9	Everton
7	Aston Villa
6	Sunderland
4	Newcastle United
4	Sheffield Wednesday

MOST SCOTTISH LEAGUE WINS (1890/91-2004/05)

51	Rangers
39	Celtic
4	Aberdeen
4	Heart of Midlothian
4	Hibernian

Success and failure

With three league titles, Huddersfield Town have been **more successful than Chelsea**! Before the 2005 title, Chelsea's only league championship crown was back in 1955.

Before the 2005/06 season, the last time a Scottish club **other than Celtic or Rangers** won the Scottish league championship was way back in 1985.

Leicester City are **the unluckiest team** when it comes to the FA Cup. They have reached the final four times, and have failed to win the trophy on each occasion.

Manchester United hold both the **biggest home** (9-0 v Ipswich Town, 1995) **and away** (8-1 v Nottingham Forest, 1999) **wins** in the Premier League.

Which city in England has won the **most league championships**? With its large number of clubs, you'd assume it was London. But you'd be wrong. The city of Liverpool, with its two clubs Everton and Liverpool, has won the league 27 times to London and Manchester's 17.

Henrik Larsson managed to be **Scotland's top scorer** in five out six seasons from 1998/99 to 2003/04.

FA CUP WINNERS

11	Manchester United
10	Arsenal
8	Tottenham Hotspur
7	Aston Villa
6	Liverpool, Newcastle United, Blackburn Rovers
5	Everton, West Bromwich Albion, The Wanderers
4	Manchester City, Wolverhampton Wanderers, Bolton Wanderers, Sheffield United
3	Chelsea, West Ham United, Sheffield Wednesday
2	Sunderland, Nottingham Forest, Preston North End, Bury, Old Etonians

MOST EXPENSIVE TRANSFERS IN ENGLISH FOOTBALL (UP TO END OF 2004/05)

PLAYER	FROM	TO	£MILLIONS
Rio Ferdinand	Leeds	Man U	30.0
Juan Sebastian Veron	Lazio	Man U	28.1
Michael Essien	Lyons	Chelsea	26.0
Didier Drogba	Marseille	Chelsea	24.0
Shaun Wright-Phillips	Man City	Chelsea	21.0
Wayne Rooney	Everton	Man U	20.0
Ruud Van Nistelrooy	PSV	Man U	19.0
Rio Ferdinand	West Ham	Leeds	18.0
Damian Duff	Blackburn Rovers	Chelsea	17.0
Michael Owen	Real Madrid	Newcastle	17.0
Hernan Crespo	Inter Milan	Chelsea	16.8
Ricardo Carvalho	Porto	Chelsea	16.5
Adrian Mutu	Parma	Chelsea	15.8
Jimmy Floyd Hasselbank	Atletico Madrid	Chelsea	15.0

GLOSSARY

Here are some of the key terms about football. There are hundreds of others, including strange terms like 'nutmeg' – when a player deliberately plays the ball between an opponent's legs – and 'onion bag' – a nickname for the goal net.

Abandoned
When a football match is called off for reasons including bad weather or problems with the crowd.

African Cup of Nations
The major competition for national teams from Africa.

A-League
The new senior league in Australia, which includes one team based in New Zealand.

Amateur
Playing football without being paid a wage.

Association Football
The full name of the game of football.

Attendance
The number of spectators who come to watch a match.

Bundesliga
The national professional football league in Germany.

Cap
The term used when a player completes a full international game for his or her country.

Champions League
The most prestigious competition for the top clubs in Europe.

Clean sheet
The term used when a team plays an entire match without letting in any goals.

Co-hosting
The term used when two or more countries share the staging of a football competition, such as the World Cup.

Continental competition
A competition either for clubs or for national teams from one particular continent of the world.

Copa America
The major competition for national teams from South America.

Copa Libertadores
The most important club competition in South America.

Debut
The term used when a player makes his or her first appearance for a club or country.

Defender
A player whose main duty is to prevent the opposing team from scoring goals.

Derby matches
Matches between teams that are intense rivals, either because they are neighbours or because they are the leading rivals in their country.

Disallowed goal
The term for a goal that is not given because a foul, offside or some other infringement of the laws of the game has taken place.

Double
This term is usually used when a club wins their country's league and the most important cup competition in the same season.

Dribbled
When the ball is moved under close control by a player's feet.

Equaliser
A goal that makes the scores in the game level.

European Championships
This is the second largest international tournament after the World Cup. Its name is often shortened to 'Euro' plus the date of the competition, such as Euro 96 or Euro 08.

European Cup
The former name of the competition for top European clubs, now known as the Champions League.

Extra-time
A way of deciding the outcome of a match in some competitions if the game ends in a draw. It involves two equal-length periods of extra play, often two times fifteen minutes.

FA
Short for the words Football Association, the organisation that runs football in a country. The first FA was founded in England.

FA Cup
The oldest surviving cup competition in football, played for by clubs in England and some in Wales, including Cardiff and Swansea.

FIFA
Short for the *Federation Internationale de Football Association*, the world governing body of soccer.

Fourth Assistant
Also known as the fourth official, a person who assists the referee and the other assistants in the running of the game.

Free transfer
The term used when a player moves to another club and no fee is paid.

Golden Boot
An award given to the player that scores the greatest number of goals at the World Cup Finals.

Golden goal
The term given to a system used in extra-time, where the first goal scored ends the game and gives the scoring team the victory.

Half-time
The interval between the first and second halves of a football match.

Hand ball
The illegal use of the hand or arm by a player.

Hat trick
In the UK, this term is used when one player scores three goals in one match.

Host
A country (or countries) that organises and stages a competition.

J-League
The professional men's football league in Japan.

Kick off
The start of the game.

La Liga
The professional men's football league in Spain.

Laws of the game
The 17 main rules for the game of soccer, established and updated by FIFA.

Le Championnat
The professional men's football league in France.

Linesmen
The old name used for the two officials now known as referee's assistants.

Mascot
This term has two meanings – it can be used for children who are selected to lead a team out on to the pitch or for fun characters used to represent a club at a match.

Midfielder
A player who tends to play further up the pitch than the defenders, but behind the strikers.

OFC Nations Cup
The competition for countries who are part of Oceania, such as Australia, Fiji and New Zealand.

Offside
A law of the game of football – a player is offside if he or she is closer to the opponent's goal than both the ball and the second-to-last opponent at the time that the ball is played.

Own goal
This is when a player scores a goal into their own team's net.

Qualifying
A match or series of matches played in order to decide which teams will play in the finals of a competition.

Penalty shootout
A series of penalties taken by two teams to determine a winner when the match ends in a draw.

Possession
The term used when a player or team have the football under close control.

Postponed
The term used when a game that was meant to be played at one time is delayed, and played instead at a later date.

Pre-season
The period before the start of the competitive season when players train and play friendly matches.

Professional
Being paid a wage to play football.

Promoted
When a team moves up one division in a league.

Red card
The card shown by a referee when a player is sent off for a serious foul, fighting or another severe infringement of the laws of the game.

Referee
The official in charge of a football match – referees run the match and have many responsibilities; any decision they make is final.

Relegated
When a team moves down to a lower division in a league.

Replay
In some competitions, when a games is drawn or abandoned, it can result in a second match being played to decide a winner – this is a replay.

Replica shirt
Shirts similar to those worn by professional players, sold to supporters.

Runners-up
The term used to describe a team that comes second in a competition or second in a football award.

Season ticket
A ticket bought by supporters that gives them entry to all their club's games in the home stadium for an entire season.

Sending off
When a player is sent from the pitch by the referee and cannot return or be replaced by another team member.

Serie A
The professional men's league in Italy.

Stadium
An arena where games of football are played.

Stoppage
A break in play during a game due to an injury or some other incident.

Striker
An attacking player whose main role is to score or create goals.

Substitute
A player who does not start a match but may be brought on during the game by the coach or manager.

Transfer fee
Money, paid by one club to another, to buy a player.

UEFA
Short for the Union of European Football Associations, this is the organisation that runs football in Europe and organises the Champions League and the European Championships.

Volley
When the ball is kicked or hit while it is in the air.

Wall
When players from the defending team stand in a row to help block a shot from a free kick it is called a wall.

Weakened side
The term used when a team does not play their strongest players, because of injuries or due to the manager or coach resting key players and giving other players a game.

Woodwork
The goalposts and crossbar.

World Cup
The biggest prize in football – almost every country in the world enters a team to play qualifying games to get the chance to play at the World Cup Finals, held once every four years.

World Player of the Year
A major award given to the best footballer of a year.

WUSA
Women's United Soccer Association – the first professional women's league.

Yellow card
The card shown by a referee to indicate that a player has been cautioned for a foul, bad behaviour or some other breaking of the laws of the game.

There are thousands of websites dedicated to the great game of football. Some are run by clubs or organisations, such as FIFA and UEFA. Other websites have been built by fans as tributes to teams, players and competitions. Here are some of the very best sites out there.

Links and pictures

http://www.soccerlinks.net /pages/index.html
A huge source of links to football websites, clearly split up into different categories.

http://www.soccer-gallery.net/gallery.php
A searchable gallery of photos and cartoons of famous footballers and teams.

http://www.footymundo.com
An excellent collection of links to other football sites, sorted by handy topics.

http://www.thisis-football.com/
A well-organised list of links to other football websites.

http://www.sporting-heroes.net/football-heroes/Default.asp
A website full of photos of football stars and biographies.

Stadiums

http://www.footballgroundguide.co.uk
A much-loved, popular website giving practical details such as directions to and descriptions of each of the 92 league grounds in English football.

http://www.stadiumguide.com
A website designed to show the leading football stadiums in Europe and across the world.

http://www.hampden park.co.uk
The official site for Scotland's greatest football stadium, Hampden Park.

http://www.groundtastic. ukgateway.net
The website devoted to the first fanzine on football grounds.

http://www.wembley stadium.com
This website features videos, 3D virtual tours and webcam shots of one of the world's most famous stadiums as it undergoes reconstruction.

Brazil hold aloft the World Cup, 1994

Official sites

www.fifa.com
The official website of FIFA, the organisation that runs world football. Check out its history pages and the details of forthcoming competitions.

http://fifaworldcup.yahoo.com/06/en
The official website for the 2006 World Cup, containing links to details of all previous World Cups.

www.uefa.com
The homepage of the Union of European Football Associations, the organisation that runs the European Championship and the Champions League.

http://www.thefa.com
Home of the English Football Association on the net, this site contains sections on the England national team, clubs and league tables and a section on the FA Cup.

http://www.scottishfa.co.uk
A website packed with information on the game in Scotland.

www.clivegifford.co.uk
The website of author, Clive Gifford, with a dedicated section on football containing quotes, links and training and playing tips.

http://www.scotprem.com
The official website of the Scottish Premier League.

http://www.soccercentral.ie
Follow players, clubs and the national team in the Republic of Ireland.

http://www.premierleague.com
The official website of the English Premier League.

http://www.irishfa.com/index
News, results and features from the official website of the Northern Ireland FA.

Clubs and players

http://www.scottishfootballrecords.com
An incredibly thorough collection of results, records and standings in Scottish football both at club and international level.

http://www.the-100.com
A list of players comprising the FIFA 100 – 100 living players selected by Pelé to celebrate FIFA's centenary.

http://www.albionroad.com
An unusual website explaining the meaning of club names in football.

http://www.footballcrests.com
Lots of information on football badges and club crests.

http://www.champions-league.org/
News, features and results of the UEFA Champions League.

http://www.pyramidfootball.co.uk
An in-depth look at the non-league scene in England with news, results and standings.

http://www.welsh-premier.com/index.php
An amazingly detailed guide to Welsh club football with profiles of grounds, clubs, players and matches.

News, facts and figures

http://www.footballsquads.com
A comprehensive statistics site showing the squads of leading teams in many European leagues and transfers organised by month and year.

http://www.european-football-statistics.co.uk
Fantastically detailed football statistics website with detail of leagues from England to Estonia and all-time rankings for teams.

http://www.eufo.de
A packed website, available in English and German, carrying details of the squads of hundreds of clubs and national teams in European football. Want to know the weight of your own team's keeper? Head here.

www.soccerbase.com
Another great statistics and results website, searchable by English and Scottish club.

http://www.tribalfootball.com
A good news site covering the big names and big games from all over the world.

INDEX

63

Acknowledgements

The publishers would like to thank the following for their kind permission to reproduce their photographs:

b=bottom; c=centre; t=top; l=left; r=right

1c Viera Rui/EMPICS; **2r** Miguelez Sports Foto/EMPICS; **3b** Studio Buzzi/EMPICS; **4r** Philippe Caron/CORBIS; **5cl** EMPICS; **5cr** Steve Morton/EMPICS; **6bc** Enrique Marcarian/CORBIS; **7tr** Matthew Ashton/EMPICS; **7c** Matthew Ashton/EMPICS; **8cl** Mike Egerton/ EMPICS; **8bl** Topham PicturePoint/ EMPICS; **9c** Matthew Ashton/EMPICS; **9bl** Andrew Milligan/EMPICS; **10br** Peter Robinson/EMPICS; **10cl** Diether Endlicher/EMPICS; **11c** Neal Simpson/EMPICS; **11tr** Reuters/CORBIS; **12r** Peter Robinson/EMPICS; **13tr** Deutsche Press-Agentur/EMPICS; **13bc** Bettmann/CORBIS; **14l** EMPICS; **15bc** Deutsche Press-Agentur/EMPICS; **15tl** Peter Robinson/EMPICS; **16bl** Matthew Ashton/EMPICS; **17cl** Matthew Ashton/EMPICS; **17tr** EMPICS; **18tr** Dusan Vranic/EMPICS; **19l** Tony Marshall/EMPICS; **19cr** Matthew Ashton/EMPICS; **20tr** Chip Beck/EMPICS; **20br** Valeria Witters/EMPICS; **20c** Tony Marshall/EMPICS; **21t** Tony Marshall/EMPICS; **22tr** Mel Evans/EMPICS; **22bl** Adam Davy/EMPICS; **23cr** Deutsche Press-Agentur/EMPICS; **23bl** Mike Egerton /EMPICS; **23tr** Matthew Ashton/EMPICS; **24tl** S&G/Alpha/EMPICS; **24cr** Peter Robinson/EMPICS; **24br** Ross Kinnaird/EMPICS; **25tr** PA Photos/ EMPICS; **25tc** Tony Marshall/EMPICS; **25cl** Peter Robinson/EMPICS; **26cr** Owen Humphreys/EMPICS; **26tl** Peter Robinson/EMPICS; **27cr** Tony Marshall/EMPICS; **27cl** Matthew Ashton/EMPICS; **28c** Ben Curtis/EMPICS; **28br** Matthew Ashton/EMPICS; **29t** EMPICS; **30c** Studio Buzzi/EMPICS; **31cr** Ross Kinnaird/EMPICS; **31tl** Matthew Ashton/EMPICS; **32cl** Mike Egerton/ EMPICS; **33l** Tony Marshall/EMPICS; **34bl** Tony Marshall/EMPICS; **34tr** Tony Marshall/EMPICS; **35br** Viera Rui/EMPICS; **36cc** Matthew Ashton/EMPICS; **38cl** Topham Picturepoint/EMPICS; **38tr** Peter Robinson/EMPICS; **39l** Matthew Ashton/EMPICS; **40cl** Matt A Brown/EMPICS; **40tr** Nick Potts/EMPICS; **41tl** Mike Egerton/EMPICS; **41br** David Jones/EMPICS; **42bl** Matthew Ashton/EMPICS; **42tr** Matthew Ashton/EMPICS; **43cr** Phil Noble/EMPICS; **44cl** Peter Robinson/EMPICS; **44tr** John Giles/EMPICS; **45l** Tony Marshall/EMPICS; **46r** Eric Lafargue/EMPICS; **47cl** Tony Marshall/EMPICS; **47cr** Tony Marshall/EMPICS; **48c** Miguelez Sports Foto/EMPICS; **49tr** John Walton/EMPICS; **49bc** Matthew Ashton/EMPICS; **50tl** Tony Marshall/EMPICS; **50cr** Anders Wiklund/EMPICS; **51l** Neal Simpson/EMPICS; **52tr** Neal Simpson/EMPICS; **52bl** Lars Moeller/EMPICS; **53br** Neal Simpson /EMPICS; **54bl** Barratts/Alpha/EMPICS; **54br** Neal Simpson/EMPICS; **55bc** Peter Robinson/EMPICS; **56c** Gareth Copley/EMPICS; **60bc** Neal Simpson/EMPICS

Jacket: Kai-uwe Knoth/AP/EMPICS; Luca Bruno/AP/EMPICS; Mike Egerton/EMPICS; Fabio Diena/EMPICS/Diena/Brengola; ABACA ABACA PRESS/ABACA/EMPICS; Scott Bales/EMPICS/Digital Sports Archive; Peter Robinson/EMPICS/Sports Photo Agency; PA/PA/EMPICS